Your Children's Ministry from Scratch

By Rev. Trisha R. Peach

ISBN: 1499273193

ISBN 13: 978-1499273199

Table of Contents

Lovingly dedicated to:

All the heroes who love Jesus and love His kids,

through glue spills, glitter messes, and goldfish cracker fights.

Underpaid, underappreciated, understaffed, overworked, overloaded.

You notice when that child misses a Sunday.

You overlook the broken chair back, because that child finally learned how to worship!

When she raised her hand to receive Christ, you cried. When he got baptized, it made your whole week.

The kids—they are why you do what you do. They are why you keep trying, even on your toughest days, because you are called to love them for Jesus' sake.

And for all you do, this book is dedicated to you.

Foreword:

"I want you to come and be our children's pastor."

This was the invitation Pastor Morrow gave me over the phone in 1971. I was just two years out of Bible College and traveling with my wife and baby daughter as a full-time evangelist specializing in children's ministry. At that point in time, there were no children's pastors in churches, so it was a surprise to get such an invitation. God had prepared me for "such a time as this." Besides my formal Bible training, I had a lot of experience in ministry to children, so this was an open door that I knew God wanted me to walk through.

During the 1970s, there was a great move in churches to establish strong ministry to children. This move helped churches grow dramatically. I soon realized that someone would need to train many others to be children's pastors. In 1977, I heard God speak to me and ask, "Who is going to fill this need?" The answer came that year when I was given the opportunity to teach a class on children's ministry at North Central University in Minneapolis. At that time I was the children's pastor in Bloomington, Minnesota, and I was able to develop a formal training program for children's pastors at the college. In 1990 I became the full-time director of the children's ministry major at the university and taught there until my retirement in 2013. It was during those years I had the opportunity to affect the lives of hundreds of young people to answer God's calling to become children's pastors.

During my years of teaching at North Central, I had the privilege of meeting many exceptional young men and women. Trisha Peach was one of these young people. Trisha has answered God's calling. She has the training, experience, and God-given talent to minister to kids and direct a strong family ministry program. Not only does Trisha do a great job in ministering to children and families, she has inspired and trained others.

The need for trained children's pastors has never been greater. God is continuing to call people to minister to children. *Your Children's Ministry from Scratch* is a must for the library of every childrens' pastor. It provides much-needed instruction and a format to assist the experienced children's pastor as well as helping those who are just now answering God's call to become children's pastors.

Dr. Dan Rector

Children's Ministry Consultant

Former Chair, Department of Children's Ministry

North Central University

Preface

My guess is that if you are reading this, you have already accepted a position in children's ministry, are actively involved in one, or are looking for practical tips to make your children's ministry fly more effectively. This book is all about the practical steps to an effective children's ministry. For the last twenty years, I have visited churches all over the United States doing kids' ministry, consulting, and many times just listening to the joys, hurts, and frustrations of kids' leaders. To write this book, I conducted two different surveys across the United States asking children's leaders to tell their stories and the lessons they have learned. If nothing else, know that you are not alone in your passion and calling to love Jesus and His kids! Why do I have this burning desire to help children's leaders? Hmmmm. Well for me it started something like this....

I vividly remember standing in the hayfield that surrounded my parents' trailer, staring at the sunset one evening the summer before I went to college. I dug the toes of my beat up sneakers into the white rocks of the gravel driveway as I prayed. I knew God had called me to minister to children, and I knew that He would make a way for me. But I was still overwhelmed at the thought that God could use a seventeen-year-old kid from a tiny town in northern Wisconsin who had no experience, no money, and no clue what God might have in store for her. I remember praying that evening: "God, I don't know why you would want to use somebody like me. You must have some better options! But God, if You will just go with me, I will go for You— anywhere, anytime. I will do whatever you ask, if You will just go with me." And He has every day, in every way.

As an eight-year-old kid at a small Bible camp, I had been praying after the service when I felt God calling me to be a children's pastor. I excitedly said, "Yes, Lord," followed immediately by, "What's a children's pastor?" Our church of seventy-five people did not have children's ministry to speak of, except for Sunday school. My eighty-three-year-old Sunday school teacher, who I dearly loved, told us the same story every week for three years (no kidding, but I will never forget it). There were no puppets, games, or anything. All around me every week was a sea of white hair. Children were not a priority at my home church, in its early years, so there were very few children. When I came home from camp excitedly blurting, "I'm going to be a children's pastor," some people smiled and said, "And next week she will want to be a princess again." I was confused about why everyone was not as thrilled as I was. Six years passed. That summer I was housekeeping at that same Bible camp, but I was really there to spy on and stalk the camp speaker—a famous children's pastor—and soak up everything he did like a sponge. I desperately prayed, "God, please confirm what You told me when I was a child. Make a way for me to learn and grow and get going on this." To my shock, on the last night of the camp, the speaker walked up to me and said, "Young lady, God has a call on your life to children's ministry, and you need to join my traveling evangelism team." I went back to my cabin that night and cried on my knees for an hour. "God you are really going to let me do this." I am still so grateful to my parents (ministers themselves) for seeing the importance and eternal significance of letting me go to do things for God. That year of kids' ministry training and travel changed my life forever. At only age fifteen, it was hard to be away from home for so long in so many new places. I was struggling to learn things like puppetry, clowning, juggling (which I never did learn), illusions, and so on. I know what it is like to be frustrated and impatient, trying to learn it "all" overnight. I didn't learn it all, and what I did learn didn't happen overnight. But I came home with an unstoppable passion for reaching kids for Christ—a passion that just couldn't wait. So I started a children's church for my home church with twelve children. Then I got together the rest of our church's teens and started a ministry team. My mom and her team did an amazing job with midweek kids' ministries. Before long, our little children's ministry began to grow. We had no specialized books to guide us, no equipment, budget, or curriculum, and usually no one to ask for advice. I learned most things the hard way, through trial and error. But this time also taught me how to put together amazing kids' ministry on little or no budget, how to work collaboratively with a team, and how to put together curriculum that has impact. What I learned—from working in that little start-up ministry all the way to being on staff at mega churches—is that the principles of children's ministry remain the same, regardless of church size or location.

At Bible college, I had an amazing mentor in Rev. Dan Rector, the chair of my department. At college I promised God that if He let me be a kids' pastor, I would help as many other kids' leaders as I could, just as someone had taken time to help me. So all these years later, I'm excited to share some tidbits of children's ministry experience from my own ministry and from ministry leaders from all over the United States. No matter how you got into kids' ministry or what led you here, God doesn't make mistakes. It is no coincidence, and the God Who led you here has great things in store for you and the kids, volunteers, and families you lead. God sets us here for "such a time as this" (Esther 4:14) So let's get started!

Chapter 1

The Road to Here: Getting Started

Myth: All other churches have a "real" kids' pastor. All other children's leaders have more education and experience in kids' ministry than me. I have no kids' ministry skills. I am totally in over my head. I cannot do this.

Truth: Stop panicking. The truth is that the majority of children's leaders I have met over the last 15 years began their ministry with no training, education, or experience in children's ministry prior to taking the position, whether volunteer or staff. Children's Ministry Academy reports, "Seventy one percent of the teacher's we've certified received NO **FORMAL TRAINING** prior to enrolling in our program."[1] So if you said yes to children's ministry and have no pastoral degree or prior experience, you are in good company. Listen to Kerri's story:

Kerri Stevens blinked twice and tried hard to swallow. Her throat was so dry, like a Dorito left on the sidewalk in summer. Her hands, still slick with sweat, were balled up into tight fists at her sides. She tried to clear her head and focus on finding her car in the church parking lot. "What just happened in there?" her mind screamed in pitches higher than hearing. Her body on total autopilot, Kerri unconsciously found her car, unlocked the driver's door with her remote, got in, and snapped her seatbelt. She sat there, hands on the wheel, staring at nothing. Her mind raged on: "This is not what I went in there for! What *did* I go in there to talk to Pastor Andersen about? How did I get myself into this?"

Kerri began to remember what brought her to church today. She needed Pastor Andersen to deal with something very important. Kerri and her husband, Chuck, had been going to Cornerstone Community Church for four years. The young couple was involved with church activities. Chuck coached the men's softball team, which

---

[1] Children's Ministry Academy, Online Certification Program 2011, http://www.childrensministryacademy.com/, (assessed March 9, 2014)

was getting better, though it hadn't won a game yet. Kerri had taken over the weekly church bulletin about a year ago. As a part-time writer for a small local paper, she had been able to use her skills to bring real quality and class to the church bulletin. This brought her a small sense of accomplishment and pride, and the good feeling of being able to contribute to the church. As a young wife, volunteer, and the mother of two girls—and working part-time—Kerri was not looking to be involved in anything else. Her plate was full. Wasn't she giving enough? The girls were involved in so much. They were the reason for the meeting with the pastor today. Only her girls—Angela, age nine and already an accomplished soccer player, and Aprille, age four and the world's greatest little ballerina—could necessitate such a difficult discussion with a pastor both Kerri and Chuck respected and loved. Kerri spent all week just getting up the courage to come in today. Chuck chickened out just a couple hours ago, as she suspected he would, with a bad headache (yeah, right). This was all so hard to do. Kerri and Chuck were not complainers. They didn't cause trouble or rock the boat. They were committed and involved and planned to stay that way. It was just… Kerri and Chuck were involved – the girls were not. The Stevens' beloved church, had but one blatant missing ingredient for their family: there was little if any ministry for their girls. And the girls did not want to go to church anymore. Kerri flinched just at the memory of the battle to get the girls into the van to go to church last Sunday. It was the same battle every Sunday. Kerri and Chuck had both dutifully sat in on a few Sunday school classes, to see if the girls were just being difficult. That was hard to imagine since the girls were always babbling with excitement on their way out the door for Girl Scouts, soccer, dance class, or school plays. Why were the church classes so unappealing for these otherwise bright, happy girls?

After ten minutes of sitting in on Angie's Sunday school class, Kerri thought the problems were clear to everyone, even the children. First of all, the rooms were very uncomfortable. All the children's classes met in the church basement, where the rooms were small and smelled of mold and old wood. The peeling yellowed paint (did it used to be white?) and the threadbare commercial carpet did nothing to cheer away the prison image from your mind. All the pictures on the walls were from her great-grandmother's time. To top it all off, the bare light bulbs did not throw much light, and the squeaky metal chairs started to dig into your hip after a few minutes.

The second problem on Kerri's list for Pastor Andersen was the awful curriculum the church was still using—or attempting to use. Why were they still reading robotically from something that was discontinued over a ten years ago? Kerri peeked at it out of morbid curiosity after class. It did not keep the kids' attention at all, nor was it age appropriate for third graders in any decade.

The third problem Kerri figured would be the toughest one for the pastor to deal with was volunteer staffing. She didn't have the whole picture yet, but she did know this: no one seemed to want to take a turn in Sonshine Church (Kerri thought "Doctrine Dungeon" might be more accurate). How many times had Pastor Andersen appealed for children's ministry volunteers from the pulpit? Monthly? Weekly? And as much as everyone seemed to love and respect their pastor, nobody seemed eager to take a turn. A year ago, he declared that every parent would have to take a turn. It sounded good in theory, but in practice some parents were taking a turn while others just ignored the rule. Some begged a different parent to take their turn, and others would just "call in sick" that morning. And the parents who did show up to teach had no training, no leader to look to for help, no helpers, and an outdated curriculum. These "weekend warriors" were understandably frustrated, uncomfortable, and just wanted to get it over with. The kids immediately picked up on that. Everything they saw, heard, and experienced said to them: "This is not important. *You* are not important. No one really wants to be here with you. So sit down and be quiet so the important adults can have church." Message received. These kids were checked out and bored, and their behavior reflected it. Some of the remaining teachers complained about the kids having "horrible attitudes" and showing "disrespect." They were kicking each other's chairs, poking each other, and making fun of the teachers behind their backs. These kids felt they "won" if they got the frustrated teacher to break and start yelling or crying. It was at least something to do. Kerri left that class knowing exactly why her girls did not want to be there. None of the kids wanted to be there. Kerri did not want to be there, and neither did the teachers. Everyone knew there were major problems with their kids' programs, but the heavy choking fog of desperation and failure seemed to permeate every part of every class. No one knew what to do, how to help, whom to ask. So no one was going to try. It wasn't that no one cared. A lot of people cared, but no one knew what to do. And no one was going to volunteer to captain this sinking ship.

If this was all so obvious to everyone else in the church, how could these difficulties escape the attention of a great pastor like Pastor Andersen? Did he notice? He had to care about their kids. Kerri and Chuck had heard people talking in low whispers at church and in their small groups. People were not happy with what was (and was not) being offered for their kids. In the back of everyone's minds were the rumors of a growing, exciting children's ministry at the "big" church ten miles over. This was the real deal—a church with a paid children's pastor, and puppets, games, leaders, outreaches, and technology. Yes, people were thinking, but most weren't leaving—yet. But with each passing week the temptation grew. Kerri and Chuck were also tempted to go but felt guilty about it. They loved their church and wanted to grow where they were planted. They loved their pastor. Hadn't he always been there when they needed him? Whenever they were sick? When Chuck was laid off three years ago? How could they just up and leave without trying something? After some careful thought, Kerri decided that perhaps Pastor Andersen didn't see the situation like the parents did. Perhaps they needed to give him the benefit of the doubt and express their concerns to him face to face and give him a chance to fix some of this! That would be only fair. He was a good man and would know how to fix the situation. So Kerri did something uncharacteristic; after two false starts, she set up an appointment for her and Chuck to meet with Pastor Andersen "about concerns with the children's ministry programs." When Chuck chickened out today, she went in anyway, because she figured she would never get up the courage to do this all over again. Now she was desperately wishing she had cancelled. How did this go so horribly wrong? What had happened in there anyway?

She had walked in with such resolve, so sure she could get her point across in a loving way, and run home happy, having done her duty. Then Pastor Andersen had looked at her from across his massive desk with his piercing yet compassionate gaze: "I hear you Kerri. I hear you."

"Um, what was I just saying?" Her palms were sweating now. Where was that unshakeable resolve again? "Pastor, for all of these reasons and more, Chuck and I, and probably several of the other parents, would really like to see this church invest more heavily in children's ministry." That was well stated, she thought. The ball is in his corner now.

"Well Kerri, I agree that these are some serious problems. And immediate action is needed. What do you think we should do about it?"

We? Who cares what I think? Well, apparently he does. "Um, well, with all of these changes that need to happen," she paused to let pastor nod in agreement, "there will have to be someone to implement them, to be responsible to make sure this all happens, that it isn't all talk." Kerri hoped that didn't sound too harsh.

To her surprise, the pastor seemed pleased. "I wholeheartedly agree. For our children's ministry to be successful, to grow, to reach our own kids more effectively we are going to need that point person, a go-to person to take it to heart and make sure this all gets done. I do care about the kids Kerri, more than you know. And these same issues have been on my mind a lot lately, and in my prayers."

Kerri sighed in relief. He did notice, and he cared. She shouldn't have relaxed so soon.

"Kerri, who do you think should be that go-to person?" he asked.

Kerri was unprepared for that question. She thought quickly about the big church ten miles away. "A children's pastor, of course."

Again the pastor had surprised her by smiling a bit and shaking his head. "When we first applied for a children's pastor at three different Bible colleges in our denomination, we had high hopes of getting one. That was five years ago."

Kerri's mouth fell open reflexively. "What is taking so long?"

"I didn't understand the whole situation at first either, Kerri. Not until they let us know that they only had about eighteen children's ministry graduates every year, and 120 churches on the waiting list."

"Oh." She tried to register that.

"And financially we are still not in any place to compete with the much larger churches on the waiting list."

"Compete?" she asked, still astounded. "Waiting list?"

"Kerri," continued Pastor Andersen, "did you know that Point Church, just ten miles from here waited more than two years to finally get a children's pastor? They have no problem paying one. There is just a serious shortage." None of this made any sense. Kerri thought there were always a lot of pastors around looking for work. Obviously, that wasn't the case with children's pastors.

"I have been praying that God would send us someone with a heart for these kids, to minister to them," Pastor Andersen said.

Kerri didn't get what he was driving at yet. "But we still don't have a children's pastor."

Pastor took a breath. "No, we don't. So maybe God is raising up someone from right here. What about you, Kerri? Can you think of anyone better? I think you would be great at it."

Oh, no. No no no. Anyone else would be better than me, Kerri thought. She frantically, desperately thrashed her brain for names. "Megan. She's a stay-at-home mom, and she's organized!" Pastor Andersen quickly responded. "She is on total bed rest with her fourth pregnancy. And they have no intention of this being their last baby, you know." Yes, the Pierces did say they wanted at least seven kids. "TJ? He loves kids."

"He has no problem teaching, Kerri, but he absolutely does not want to be in charge. He is pretty disorganized too. Can you honestly see him in charge?"

Kerri grimaced as she silently remembered having to fill in for TJ three weeks ago when he "accidently" slept in. Another time he somehow lost the entire donkey costume two weeks before the Christmas play. Never did find it, either. Maybe he would be a poor choice. "Amber?"

"I believe her exact words to me were, 'I would rather have a root canal than speak up front.' She would never go for that. She is way too shy," he said matter-of-factly.

Kerri didn't argue that one. Amber didn't even come to church if she thought that she might be called up front, like on Mother's Day. "What about Miriam and her husband, Ken?"

The pastor looked at Kerri with shock. She was definitely reaching this time. "Kerri, Ken and Miriam are pushing eighty. Ken is on blood-pressure medication and had a small stroke last year. Miriam is so frail and getting more forgetful by the day. Physically, they are not in any shape to…"

"There *must* be someone else. Anyone else!" she practically shrieked.

"Someone that you would want your kids learning from?" Pastor Andersen was winning and he knew it. Kerri was silent as she stewed on that one. The pastor smelled blood in the water and went for the kill. Leaning across his ridiculously massive desk, waiting until she met his gaze, loving Pastor Andersen looked into Kerri's burning red face and said with such sincerity, "Kerri, if God put this on your heart, and it bothered you enough to come here today, don't you think perhaps He wants *you* to do something about it?" She thought she was going to throw up. She wished she could throw up so she would have an excuse to run for the bathroom and then out the front door. Why were there no fire exits in this room? And there he was. Still looking at her so fatherly with all that patience. She had to force her mouth to spout out an answer. It was only right to let him down easy.

"Will you try heading up the children's ministries department for three months and just see if you like it?"

No way, she thought. "All right. I can do that." What had just come out of her mouth?

"Wonderful!" Pastor Andersen was ecstatic. "I think you will make a great children's director for our church."

A what? Me? A children's director? What did I just commit too?

"Well this has been such a great session together, Kerri. God is doing great things. Let's close in prayer together." Close? Wait, what just happened? "God, thank you for raising up a person from within our congregation with a heart for the souls of our kids…" Kerri didn't hear the rest. In her heart she desperately and deeply prayed. "Jesus, come quickly! Yea, though I walk through the valley of the shadow of death, I will fear no evil…"

Kerri looked up from the steering wheel. How long had she been sitting there? What was the question that was rooting her in her place with fear? What just happened in there? Kerri knew that now she was stuck. She had just committed to three months of this. But the thought that consumed her now was this: how would she survive the next three months? Where do I start? What now?

YOUR STORY: Kerri's story may not be very different from your own. In my years in children's ministry, in all my travels, this was a recurrent topic of conversation with the leaders in almost every church: The shortage of children's pastors has not gotten any better. If anything, it may be even worse. Churches are growing larger, reaching for higher standards of technology and excellence. And on the flip side, as our culture becomes more and more child-centered, families are expecting age-appropriate ministry for their kids at your church. In fact, according to Pastor Leith Anderson, author of *Dying for Change*, "The old top three factors families used to choose a church were 'location, pastor, and denomination.' Not so anymore. Today the new top three are 'location, pastor, and children's ministry'."[2] And Vanderbloemen Search Group puts it this way, "One of the primary characteristics we see in churches that are not thriving is a stagnant or failing children's ministry. If the kids dislike going to church, parents will simply not put up with the kicking and screaming. On the other hand, one of the fastest ways to ensure families become a part of your church is to develop a world-class Children's Ministry."[3]

---

[2] Leith Anderson, "Children Are #3," *Enrichment* journal, Spring 1999, 24.
[3] Danny Waterson, Vanderbloemen Search Group, "Why High Capacity Children's Pastors are So Hard to Find" http://www.vanderbloemen.com/insights/why-high-capacity-childrens-pastors-are-so-hard-to-find, July 2014, accessed July 2014

And it doesn't seem to me that our colleges are producing any more children's pastors than they were a decade ago. We have to ask a

 few important questions: If the biggest churches struggle to find a kids' pastor, does God care about the kids in the small or medium-size churches? Of course, He does. Then why is He not raising up leaders for these kids without a children's pastor? I believe God is raising up these leaders. Not people who are perfect or even people who can work a puppet. God is raising up people who love God and love His kids. They see the problems in children's ministry and can't sit back and take it anymore. Many current children's ministry leaders are moms and dads, grandparents, business executives, lawyers, truck drivers, drama majors, and writers to name a few. What they all have in common is a love for the kids in their church, and the sense that "something must be done about this" (what Bill Hybels would call a holy discontent).

If you are reading this book, then you must be seeing the undeniable importance of children's ministry. And perhaps you are one

of the many who "fell" into this position because you wanted to help, no one else would do it, the pastor asked you to, and so on. But I do not believe you are where you are by accident. Scripture tells us the "steps of a righteous man are ordered from the Lord." Most new children's directors tell me the same things: "I can't do this. They have the wrong person. I can't work a puppet. What am I going to do?"

Let me answer this loud and clear right from the first chapter of this book: firebrand juggling, acrobatics, and harmonica solos, though pretty awesome, are not prerequisites to doing a great job as a kids' leader (see chapter 9 on the illustrative methods). Whether you are at a church of thirty or a church of thirty thousand, whether you are always planning to work in kids' ministry or were "thrown in," when God calls, He equips.

What are the key areas to focus on when starting or revamping a children's ministry program? Here are three great tips on getting your kids' ministry started from scratch.

I. Start with what you know. One pastor put it to me this way: use what is in your hand. Moses had his staff, the boy had his lunch of five loaves and two fish, Elijah had his cloak, and Lydia had her business selling purple cloth. God used them in a powerful way with what they already had. What skills do you already possess?

Circle all that apply:

Administrative skills, up-front speaking skills, writing, organizing, making people feel included, making up games, media giftings storytelling, teaching, praying for others.

What "secular" skills do you bring from your profession?

_____

_____

_____

_____

Know what you bring to the table, and recruit leaders alongside you who have different but complementary gifts to create a balanced team.

What are your greatest strengths and talents?

_____

_____

Write down a few ideas about how to use those strengths and talents in children's ministry, children's classes, or working with volunteers and parents. For example: "I have skills as an accountant. I could write a budget and organize a VBS or other outreach for our kids' ministry." "I have tech skills. I could update our media software for the kids' areas."

_____

_____

Keep these ideas in mind, perhaps revisit them, and write new ones down the road.

II. Step two in kick starting your children's ministry from scratch: Find the right training. There is great children's ministry training out there that is better than ever before. Here are some places to start:

A. Traditional Bible Colleges—A Bible college used to be the only place, short of traveling with a kids' pastor or evangelist, to find training or experience in children's ministry.

The pros:

1. Collective Experience—A Bible College that offers a children's ministry degree is the gold standard for learning about kids' ministry. You benefit from the years of experience your professors bring to the table, the best textbooks, and the latest in cutting-edge ideas.

2. Collaboration—The greatest edge you gain at a traditional Bible College training is the chance to collaborate and network with other kids' ministry leaders and professors. Those connections and networks are not just a benefit while you are in school. These connections provide you with a support system and an idea think tank throughout your ministry career. (I am still friends with many of the people I went to school with). Do not underestimate the value of learning together with passionate people who are dedicated to ministry.

3. Connection Opportunities—Children's ministry is all about who you know and where you have served. Traditional Bible Colleges have the advantage of (usually) helping you find internships in churches and opportunities serving alongside the best kids' pastors out there. Trust me on this: experience always trumps. A church will choose quality experience over any other training out there. If you get a chance to be mentored, to serve with an experienced children's pastor, take that opportunity for the precious gift it is. It will change your life, I promise, and you'll learn more than you could in two hundred years in the classroom.

The cons:

1. Distance—The biggest deterrent to a children's ministry program at a traditional Bible College is proximity. If you are already being asked to lead in your church's children's ministry, then leaving home, going far away to study for four to six years may not be an option. You may already be married and have kids and a career to think about. More than likely you do not have a traditional Bible College close to home. But by all means, please check.

2. Lack of Quality Programs—If you do have a Bible college near you, it probably does not offer a children's ministry degree. And if it does, check into the quality of the program. When was the curriculum written? Are new, cutting-edge ideas being taught? What is the experience level of the professors? The likelihood of finding a quality program near your home is small. Many churches would love to get their children's leaders the training they need, but they fear that nothing is available nearby. And they cannot bear the thought of parting with their leaders for several years!

3. Time—The length of time it takes to complete the courses (see above). It is four to six years full time. If you can

only study part time, you are looking at eight or more years. Jesus said to sit down and count the cost before you act. It is a good idea to think this part through before you start a course of education. Especially when you factor in...

4. Cost—At the writing of this book, most pastors borrow an average of twenty to forty thousand dollars to complete their degree. This enormous debt keeps many pastors from full-time ministry until the debt is paid down.[4] When looking into the cost of traditional Bible college, be sure to investigate scholarships and grants. I know students who were able to graduate debt-free on scholarships and grants; it is not impossible, but it takes a lot of preplanning and work. Talk to pastors who were able to graduate with little debt and also to the college's financial aid department. Bottom line: traditional Bible colleges are the gold standard, and their cost reflects that.

B. Online Children's Ministry Degrees—This is a relatively new option. But a children's pastor friend of mine had a good experience with this. She started working full time at a massive church

---

[4] Bill Silva-Breen, Financial Aid Director, Luther Seminary, "Understanding the Impact of Student Debt," http://www.luthersem.edu/scholarships/debt_impact.aspx, (assessed May 2014)

at age eighteen, so a full-time college residency was not an option for her. While working at the church, she studied for a twelve-month certificate from Children's Ministry University Online. She finished it last June and was really happy with the program. She is now going to pursue an associate's and official credentialing. Other online kids' ministry courses are available from Liberty University Online, and Children's Ministries Institute, a training program from Child Evangelism Fellowship. I am hopeful that this type of study will soon grow and expand.

C. Regional Training—My denomination offers regional training in children's ministry at little or no cost, depending on the state. Call your denomination's state office and ask what might be available in the way of training, for you and your team, whether or not you are an "official" children's pastor or not. If your denomination doesn't offer anything, consider calling some other denominations in your state; some children's ministry organizations offer seasonal or regional trainings that anyone can attend.

III. Get connected and networking, and do it now. I don't care if you are the most amazing rock-star children's pastor God ever created, we are always better together than in a one-person show. One of the best moves I made early in my career was joining a kids' ministry Google group and later a kids' ministry Facebook page for my region. We shared ideas, warned others about our mistakes, shared our best illustrations, and even traded actual sets, props and other equipment (which will cut your expenses). We found ways to work together on outreach and collaborate on training. I was amazed at how much more we could conquer together.

Here is what Pastor Dave Robertson, children's pastor for more than a decade, has to say about networking:

I have 2 cents worth to say about being connected. I would say that someone just starting out should join networks of children's ministry people immediately. For starters: (a) 1 interdenominational network of kids' pastors (b) 1 district-wide network in your denomination (c) 1 regional interdenominational network. If there isn't a network, sometimes it doesn't take too long to start them.

Also, sign up for national networks such as cmconnect.org through INCM.org. Point being here is to get connected. From here you gain insights. Even more importantly, you can save valuable time and money by connecting with people who have already written many publications that help administrate a children's ministry. You can get free curriculum and resources from children's pastors. These can be from file sharing to actual products. A new CP (children's pastor) doesn't want to spend the first 5 years developing a volunteer training manual, complete with policies forms, etc. (like I did), if you can just customize one that your fellow CP emails. A new person doesn't want to be stuck at the computer. He/she wants to be out meeting people and recruiting. The faster he/she can get past the figure-it-out phase or the "administrative season of focus," the better. For those who are in it alone at the start, it is a big deal. A new children's pastor doesn't have time to re-invent the wheel. - Pastor Dave

All children's leaders start somewhere. Now that you are on your way, leading with what you know, getting the training, and getting connected, it's time to move forward with the big thing that will kick-start and propel everything else in your kids' ministry now and for years to come. What is it? Buying a bunch of stuff? Fitting into skinny jeans? Dusting off that unicycle? Nope, at least not yet. Before anything else, there must be...

Chapter 2 Vision Check

Who Is Driving This Thing Anyway?

From the time I was a small child, I have always had to wear big, thick glasses. Like the Coke-bottle kind, with bifocals, and all that other stuff that really gets you beat up in the third grade. No wonder I am in children's ministry. I will never forget something AMAZING that happened the year I turned thirteen. I had saved my lawn-mowing and babysitting money for months and finally had enough for my first pair of contact lenses. I remember being nervous about the eye exam and stuffing those things into my eyes the first time. But I was a determined and motivated middle-schooler who was more than prepared to camp out at Wal-Mart all night if that's what it took to get those contacts in. No wimping out now. It only took three tries, and when I spun around in the chair, what I saw took my breath away. At first I couldn't speak. I didn't recognize myself in the mirror. As I looked out into the store, everything was so sharp and clear. Light was everywhere and colors were so vibrant! I went from being nearly legally blind in heavy glasses to better than 20/20 in a moment. I considered myself a tough girl, but tears were filling my eyes (scaring the eye doctor), but I was overwhelmed at how full of light the world was. I was astonished at how much I had been missing. So much was clear to me now. And it started with a vision check.

Most people have no idea how bad their eyesight is until they make that appointment and go to the eye doctor. Most are surprised by how much better they see with glasses or contacts. The same is usually true for churches. As leaders, most of us are completely unaware of how "bad" our vision has become, just how much we are missing the mark, until we bite the proverbial bullet and do that vision check. So, fellow children's leader, how's your vision doing? For the children's ministry at your church, I mean. What does it matter? Vision is everything. It is the basis of everything else—budget, recruiting, and team building. "Without a vision, the people perish" (Prov. 29:18). This chapter is intentionally toward the beginning of the book because it is the foundation for all the chapters that follow. Let me show you what I mean.

I routinely consult with churches trying start a new kids' ministry or revamp one that has stagnated. I always ask this question: "Tell me your vision for this kids' ministry. Share with me your heart for these kids and families?" I typically get a weird look and one of these answers which I like to call:

Myths of Kids' Church Vision

Children's leader: "Ummmm, well, I am just holding down the fort until we get a real children's pastor."

My thoughts: Many churches wait YEARS to get a children's pastor. That is a long time to put your kids, families, and church in a holding pattern. What a terrible waste of resources and precious formative years. Most children are forming all of their ethical worldview before age twelve, and their church is silent to them in this crucial window. Inexcusable!

Children's leader: "Survive. I just hope we can survive another week, and keep the classrooms open, and no one else quits."

My thoughts: A survival mentality has the stench of death all over it. "Just surviving" isn't living, and it isn't vision. No one wants to be a part of the First Church of Barely Hanging On. Not the new leaders, the current leaders, the parents, the kids, and not even you. Whatever happened to being "more than conquerors through Christ Who loved us," and "He gives us everywhere we set our feet," and "life, more abundantly"? Please believe that "Surviving andholding the fort are equivalent to putting a Band-Aid on an amputation and awaiting a slow death. Everyone in the church knows it. They are all just waiting for someone to arrive and save the situation. "Someone" is going to need a big vision, and faith in an even bigger God.

Children's leader: "I'm just so happy no one got hurt this week. We aim to give them back to the parents in one piece and call it a day"

My thoughts: AHHHHHHHHH! (Insert slamming head into wall here.) A whole hour and no one died. Is this the only goal? Lowered expectations! Have you ever considered how little time we have to effect change in the lives of these kids and families? Well, let's face facts a moment. Each year we have 52 weekends. And statistics tell us that the average American family attends church about 1.4 times a month.[5] It breaks down to less than two hours per month with each child, which gives you around 17 services a year (not counting midweek). Then subtracting special services like Easter and Christmas, and accounting for weather-related absences, you are down to maybe 14 services a year. Think about that: only 14 hours a year to make a lasting impact in a child's life! That tears me up inside. Why then do we waste even a moment on games that have no meaning and do not tie into the message? Why waste so much time on snacks? Why have any time-fillers at all? Our teams made a choice long ago to enforce the number one rule: no dead time ever. What this means is no games, snacks, empty time, crafts, or anything else unless it directly ties into the message. Every moment, every second is carefully crafted to have maximum impact in reaching and keeping our kids for Christ. For over a decade now, we have struggled to stay within the allotted time. We run over a lot of weeks, just trying to get every second of ministry into these kids. There's absolutely no time to waste on "fluff."

I sat in the back row of a kids' service at a large church a few years ago. They had invited me to observe, to try to see why their ministry wasn't growing and no one wanted to volunteer. To my horror, the leaders began by throwing a bucket of candy on the floor, and all

---

[5] Rebecca Barnes and Linda Lowry, "Seven Startling Facts About Church Attendance in America,"www.churchleaders.com/pastors/pastor-articles/139575-7-startling-facts-an-up-close-look-at-church-attendance-in-america.html, (assessed April 2014)

the children were rooting around the floor like animals, pushing and shoving each other (several getting hurt) and fighting over the candy. They stretched this out for twenty minutes. Then, not knowing what else to do, they put in a video for the last seventy minutes. This was a church that had the budget, the curriculum, quality people, and first-rate facilities and equipment. But it lacked the most important component of all: strong leadership and vision. It remains one of the most painful ninety minutes of my life. Today the church has turned that children's ministry around and continues to be an inspiring success story. The key to the turnaround was establishing vision and clear direction.

Children's leader: "We just gotta keep them quiet, sitting still, and not acting up! Quiet, still and not in trouble!"

My thoughts: I have trouble not acting up in that kind of environment! Of course they are going to act up. They pick up on the fact that they are being babysat—not engaged. The older ones will start acting out first, and the younger ones will always mirror what they see the older ones doing. Right now in the United States, we are losing the vast majority of our Christian kids from the faith BEFORE they even reach 18 years of age. According to the Barna Group's extensive research findings, "Nearly three out of every five young Christians (59%) disconnect either permanently or for an extended period of time from the church life after age 15."[6] "What does that mean? It means that of the good, church going kids in YOUR kid's church right now, most of them will never ever darken a church door again once they reach the age of 18. Ken Hamm, Britt Beemer, and Todd Hillard also explore this growing problem in their 2009 book *Already Gone: Why your kids will quit church and what you can do to stop it* (Master Books). Their research not only agrees with Barna, they found, "Only 11 percent of those who have left the Church were still attending during the college years. Almost 90 percent of them were lost in middle school and high school. By the time they got to college they were already gone! About 40 percent are leaving the Church during elementary and middle school years!"[7]

Can you look the kids in your group in the eye and pick three out of five of them to turn their backs on God? I cannot bear that thought. I literally cried when I read that statistic. When on earth did losing the vast majority of our kids become okay? Who ever thought this was okay with God? If you had a hospital in your area that lost three out of every five of its patients, how long would that hospital be allowed to operate? And what about the one or two kids out of five who

---

[6] David Kinnaman, Barna Group, *Why Young Christians are Leaving the Church and Rethinking Church, 2011, https://www.barna.org/teens-next-gen-articles/528-six-reasons-young-christians-leave-church*

[7] Ken Hamm, Britt Beemer, and Todd Hillard, *"Already Gone: Why your kids will quit church and what you can do to stop it"* (Christian Book Distributors) 2009 https://answersingenesis.org/christianity/church/already-gone/

do stay in the church for life? I am convinced we do too good of a job making sure they always stay quiet, sit still, and never act. What I mean is that the kids who do end up staying in church, often have little idea how to serve the church as an adult. They become churched adults who are great at sitting silently doing nothing.

The definition of insanity is doing the same thing over and over and expecting a different result. Something has to change. Don't underestimate the impact of one man or woman passionate for God with a big vision. How would our churches change across this country if we started really engaging our kids, not wasting a minute, and treating it as their church, their service? What if we started expecting more of our kids? The public school already does. They are leaders in their sports groups as young as nine. What if we intentionally created a culture in which kids became servant leaders and serving Jesus and His church was the norm? The churches doing so are keeping more of these kids in junior and senior high school, on into college, and beyond. And what's more, they keep going in their leadership and serving. They are world changers! How do you engage your kids more and more in serving? More on that later. For right now, decide in your heart that you will have a big vision to help kids learn their gifts, learn to serve, and learn to lead.

A note about vision: Who is in the driver's seat? Have you ever had a heated discussion during a long car ride about who is driving and who is navigating? Doesn't it get on your nerves when someone in the car forgets who is in which role (that is, a back-seat driver)?

I have seen this in a vehicle and even more so within the church. When you need to make a decision about curriculum, space, sets, equipment, and so on, what is the major determining factor in making that decision? Too many would answer budget or administration. Growing churches that are reaching lots of people for Jesus have realized that vision, not budget or administration needs to be in the driver's seat. Everything else is a guideline to help you navigate. Your shoes don't get to tell your feet how big to grow. For example, when choosing a curriculum, you may have to pass over the cheaper one because it doesn't line up with your church's vision and values. If one of your current church values is ministering to the whole family, but your curriculum does not have any part that engages the family, then VISION TRUMPS- meaning, you have to change your curriculum to match your vision, not vice-versa. If one of your values is outreach to the community, and one of your leaders is "weighing anchor" and having a bad attitude about outreach, vision trumps. That leader will have to be worked with, or perhaps even removed from that area of ministry. Too often we make vision ride strapped in the back, in a rear-facing infant seat. And what happens when we let budget, administration, or even people's feelings dictate all decisions in the church? You don't go anywhere. You stay safe and sound. You don't grow, and you don't leave the parking lot. Your children's ministry is, for all intents and purposes, gone, stagnated, and "parked."

For a church to grow and change the world for Jesus, vision and administration must work together. But vision must be in the driver's seat. It comes first, and when a decision has to be made, vision trumps.

So how should a church start the process of devising and articulating a vision for this kids' ministry? This is exciting stuff! Let's look at the steps to developing a great kids' ministry vision.

1. Pray daily and ask others to pray for you. Begin to journal what God is showing you for the kids' ministry in your church.

2. Memorize your church's mission statement. Churches tend to use the terms *vision* and *mission* interchangeably, so follow suit with what they are doing. For example, if your church has a "ministry mission," then the children's area would have a "ministry mission." It is important that the children's mission statement be in line, in perfect sync with the overall mission and direction of the church. For example, if the church's mission statement says, "Reaching, teaching, and loving our city for Jesus," then the kids' mission statement should say, "Reaching, teaching, and loving the kids of our city for Jesus." What would this mean? Everything you do in kids' ministry needs to fall under that statement. Are you reaching new kids with the message of salvation? Are you effectively teaching them about God and His Word? How are you showing the love of Jesus to the kids of your city? Here is one that doesn't work. The church mission statement says, "Come as you are, leave different." The kids' mission statement says, "Instructing our children in the love of our Lord and Savior Jesus the Christ, keeping them unspotted from the world. Amen." See how those two just don't mesh together? These vision statements must flow together. Make sure you have your lead pastor's approval and guidance on this.

3. Read vision statements from kids' churches all over the country. Yes, the internet just got more awesome. Do not plagiarize another church's vision statement. Look for ideas of how to phrase what God is laying on your heart.

4. Work with a team. Carefully select key volunteers who have spent time in the ministry, and include a staff member and a parent or two. Write their job descriptions, and (without letting anyone take over) seek their input and ideas. I have had great names for kids' services and outreaches result from these brainstorming sessions. The best part is that you will more than likely have their full support when you start making changes to the ministry. They will be your biggest cheerleaders, and their excitement will create momentum and assist with recruiting.

5. Set a few goals for your first year. Notice I said *a few*. Goal-setting is an important part of any ministry. If you are like me, you may want to "get in there and fix all this" in ten days. It won't work that way. When I started as children's pastor at my last church, I saw some severe problems right away with curriculum, programs, staffing, and more. I cannot express how badly I wanted to jump in and fix every problem that first week. I was beyond disappointed when my boss said (paraphrasing Andy Stanley), "Trish, this ministry is more of a barge—

a huge ship—not a canoe. If you try to turn this thing that tight, not only are we going to capsize (turn out weak programs, thin communication, less than excellent serving opportunities), but worse, we will have a lot of volunteers who will not make this turn with you. You need to get them on board with the vision first, before radically turning this ship. Think, plan, and vision cast first." As irritating as it was to wait (I think I almost exploded twice), the truth is that he was right. The time we took to pray, plan, dream, and communicate meant that several months later we launched a quality program with excellent opportunities and a lot of parent support. Best of all, almost all of our leaders made the turn and were fully onboard with the new vision and direction of the children's ministry. We had set a direction, and gained a team. Within eleven, months the children's ministry had quadrupled. That is the power of vision, the power of a team. Set a few goals for your mile markers along the way.

6. Conduct research on the culture your church is trying to reach. I was surprised to find that the conservative, polka-loving city of my second kids' pastorate had a very low crime rate, but it was the number one city in the nation for alcoholism and the third for depression. Over half of all the kids in my ministry were from homes where parents were divorced or remarried. This was important for me to know in

developing our outreaches, curriculum, and more. What do you know about the culture of where you live? Don't guess. Find out. What are these kids facing on a daily basis? What are the schools like? Is it a community of working-class homes? Wealthy homes? The inner city? How many different ethnicities live there? Everything looks different when your vision is clearer. See the kids God is giving you. They are not generic; they are not textbooks. They are kids. And just because you grew up in an area means nothing. Many of these kids have gone through more in ten years then you or I will go through in a lifetime. This is not the same world in which we grew up. Know your audience and what they like, how they talk, what they listen to, the games they play, what they watch, and what they are thinking about. Even the Apostle Paul said, "I have become all things to all men, that by any means I may save some." Go get to know your audience. What do they need to know and hear? One children's pastor I know complained that the kids were "checked out" on her whole series about "the abundant life." Then she learned that almost a fourth of the families in her church were facing foreclosure or the fear of losing their homes after a GM plant in their area closed. She changed her messages to "God cares about you, He will take care of you, He listens when you pray." Now she had their total attention. She was addressing them where they were. Hands went up all over the room with questions (they ran out of time for all of them), and some stayed behind for prayer, tears streaming down their faces. It's not about rotely droning through a curriculum and rejoicing, "Yay, no one died." Vision trumps. Is your vision big enough and clear enough?

So how do you come up with those first few goals? That is a huge question, and here are steps you can take to establish them:

1. Pray.

2. Obtain input from your lead pastor and, if available, your church's senior leadership

3. Look at the mission statements of your church and kids' ministry. Ask, what steps do we need to take now to accomplish the overall vision of the church?

4. Ask yourself these questions and write out your responses: What are the greatest needs facing the children and families in our community right now? How can we better meet those needs? What are the three biggest problems in our kids' ministry right now?

Here are sample responses to the questions in steps 4 and 5:

Church's mission statement: "Reaching the world, one soul at a time."

Children's mission statement: "Reaching families, one child at a time."

What are the greatest needs in our community?

A. Many children in our community are going hungry in the summer without school lunches.

B. Less than 45 percent of our community goes to any church regularly.

C. More than half of the children in our kids' ministry are from single-parent homes, and the parent is working full time.

How can we better meet these needs?

a. We could help feed hungry families in the summer

b. We need outreaches, serving opportunities geared toward giving us a bigger voice in the community

c. We could find ways to support and assist single parent families

What are the biggest needs in our kids' ministry right now?

    A.   More volunteers.

    B.   Better curriculum.

    C.   Better visitor follow-up.

Our goals for this year:

    A.   We will recruit 16 more volunteers to serve regularly in our kids' ministry.

    B.   We will offer 3 new serving opportunities this year: community days in the summer, feeding families, and sports camp or a VBS.

    C.   We will offer specific resources for single parents at no cost: books, babysitter lists, parenting classes, and so on.

    D.   We will form a four-person volunteer team to research curriculum. We will choose a curriculum by May 3.

    E.   We will recruit a volunteer to answer to this staff person: _____. This volunteer will follow up on all visiting families, making connections with them, setting up visitor packets, and making sure we obtain new family information at check-in.

See the progression of how these flow together? You can easily see if you hit the mark or not. Everything else—curriculum, budget, and so forth—comes out of this planning.

Once you establish the vision and goals for the kids' ministry, clearly communicate them to the congregation the vision and goals. Andy Stanley, in his book *7 Habits of Effective Ministry* calls this "clarifying the win." Does everyone on your team know what a winning weekend kids' service looks like? Take them to see one. Take them to a church that is doing what you want to do. Take them to a conference. Watch a great kids' service online. Make sure everyone knows the goals, the vision, and how to know if you are "winning." Is a win that we didn't dirty up the carpet this week? Is it a win if we "survived," or if "no one died"?

Or is the win that kids opened up and asked hard questions, that they are finally learning how to worship, or that more kids than ever participated in fine arts? Three kids "got it" and finally understood salvation! Whatever the goal is, don't assume that everyone on your team knows the goals and is on the same page, especially if they were "holding down the fort" a long time. Write out the goals for your whole team to see, and make sure to celebrate your progress. Talk about each win, email your team, post the pictures on Facebook (with permission)—celebrate. It will ignite, solidify, and grow your team. Everyone wants to be on a team that is winning.

I will close this chapter with an earth-shattering exercise, one that I have done many times with my teams. Visualize your church, five years from now. Picture yourself pulling up to the parking lot and driving down the driveway. What do you see? What has changed? Where do the children's ministry leaders park? Now you walk into the building. What door are you using? Now walk into the kids' area. What do you see? What do you hear? What is going on in the kids' area before and during the service? How are you feeling? Is it dark, light, loud? What is different now? Take a minute to think about the kids' ministry at your church in five years, then write down what you saw. I promise that you will want to refer back to this later.

_____

_____

_____

_____

_____

_____

_____

_____

_____

These don't have to be perfect right now, but let's get started. Let's work on a sample vision statement for your children's ministry.

Write down your church's overall vision statement:

_____

_____

Write a sample kids' ministry statement:

_____

_____

What three things would you like to see change in the next twelve months of kids' ministry at your church? Be specific and write measureable goals. Don't write, "I hope we get volunteers." Instead write, "We will recruit 10 more elementary volunteers." Instead of, "Kids' church won't be so crazy," write, "We will launch a new curriculum for kids' church." The goals don't have to be perfect right now. The point is to give your team something to shoot for.

1._____

2._____

3._____

Sometimes what we *stop* doing is just as important as what we *start* doing. Based on your vision statement, list three things the ministry will stop doing in the next twelve months: (Examples might be, leaving trash all over the hallways; showing videos for longer than 10 minutes; having dead time when the kids come in etc.)

1. _____

2. _____

3. _____

Feel free to return to these lists to tweak and correct the goals. But I hope God is speaking to you through these exercises to dream big. These are His kids, after all. Everything else we will learn comes back to your vision. Check it frequently. If it doesn't require God, then you are not thinking big enough. So let's move on, and happy dreaming.

Chapter 3

Budget Is Not a Swear Word

Say that word again Mr. Peepers and you'll be snacking on a bar of soap

As I roll over in my bed and blink at the daylight streaming in the window, I hit the snooze alarm for the first of twelve times. But then, I realize, this is it! The day is finally here! The day I have been waiting for and anticipating all year long. As I spring out of bed and throw on my lucky red jeans, the birds are singing around my head, and I know in my heart, this will be the day I write—the best budget of all time! Said no children's pastor ever.

Writing budgets is not my favorite things to do. But over the years I have developed a much deeper appreciation for what a budget can do for a ministry. While you may not look forward to writing your budget with the same fervor as doing a VBS or an Easter Egg Outreach, the best kids' leaders realize that a well-written budget is equally important to a strong ministry. However, there are many myths about budgets and kids' ministry.

Budget Myth #1: We do not and never will have a children's ministry budget because our church has no money for it.

Truth: I am about to explode a land mine up in here. The truth is that EVERYTHING needs a budget. Every family, every volunteer organization, every vacation and your kids' ministry. "But Pastor Trish, our church has no money for kids' ministry. Really we have none." Every church I talk to says that, and it hasn't been true yet. Exactly how much is your church spending annually on curriculum, paper, snacks, supplies, and videos? Have your ever checked into it? Most kids' leaders have never taken a very close look at what the church is already spending on kids.

Your first step in developing a budget for your children's ministry is to find out what the church is spending on kids. What is it spending on youth and small groups? Most churches will give you a complete copy of their fiscal budget upon request. If the children's ministry at your church has been weak, stagnant, or without vision and direction, do not be surprised if the money being spent is minimal. Every ministry has to start somewhere. Find out what is actually being spent now. I have not yet encountered a church that is spending absolute zero and refuses to even consider changing that. If a church decides not to invest anything in its kids, then it is already a dying church, and money alone is not going to change that. That is a vision problem. However, too many kids' leaders jump to the conclusion that their church will never have a kids' ministry budget. Don't give up just yet.

Budget Myth #2: Our church will not give anything to the kids' ministry because they do not care about the kids. I am the only one in this church who cares about these kids. They only care about and give money to the youth ministry/worship ministry/outreach ministry, and so on. That will never ever change.

Truth: Holy martyr syndrome, Batman! This mentality comes right out of the survival thinking we addressed in chapter 1. I need to tell you a secret: budget dollars follow vision. No vision, no budget. It is the unspoken secret of churches everywhere. The area of the church that is pulling the biggest momentum, success (according the church's definition of a "win"- that is important), biggest sections of the church.....and.......biggest NUMBERS ends up with the largest portions of the budget. The National Children's Ministry director for my denomination told us in a conference, "Numbers of people do matter in every budget in a church." Did you just scream unfair? Is it really that unfair? Is it FAIR to keep pumping the church's limited resources into dying programs that are "surviving" on life support, with no plan to pull up? It is the age old question of which comes first: the budget or the growth? Kids' pastors often tell me, "If I just had a lot of money, this could grow and grow, but they won't let me." Many times that youth pastor you are envying came in with a huge vision, saw it start going and growing, and the church's budget got behind that vision, which fueled it to greater heights. The short answer here is that growth precedes budget dollars. If you show that you can be responsible with what you have, your church will be more likely to trust you with more resources (parable of the talents). Credibility and respect are earned, not demanded by virtue of the position. Show your work. Create a kids' ministry that has quality and vision and impact. Create a kids' ministry your church will want to support!

A word about changing culture and church budgets: When "youth ministries" first started taking off in the 1970s, they were crazy popular and some grew lightening fast. Churches changed budgets to reflect that, putting large chunks of money and resources into that area. Children's ministry as we know it came a bit later, blossoming in the 1980s. Some churches simply have never changed their way of thinking since the 1970s, that is: Step 1: Get a senior pastor, pay him the most. Step 2: Get a youth pastor, pay him and his department the second most. Step 3: Get a children's leader, pay him or her the least. I do have to admit that this thinking is out there, and it makes no sense. Why? Well the biggest reason for churches to rethink the way they budget is.......

The culture of our world has changed. Many years ago, families were primarily two-parent homes that were led by the parents, driven by the parents' schedules, and catered to the needs of the parents and their jobs. Children were to be "seen and not heard" and in many ways subservient to adults. Churches followed the dictates of the culture. Services were led by adults, driven by parents' schedules, catering to the needs of adults and their jobs.What is different today? The biggest difference I see is that most families live in what I call child-driven homes. Today's average home is a single-parent or blended-family home, led by caretakers of children, driven by the children's schedules (soccer, hockey, piano lessons, ballet, speech meets, etc.). The home revolves around the children's school, music, clubs, hobby and sports schedules. Much of the household budget goes to the child's perceived needs and desires. According to the American Psychological Association, the average American mom reports being completely overwhelmed with stress almost all of the time (see . The parents we see every week live like that. I remember talking to one mom who was so stressed. I asked her, "What is there in your life that you can drop right now to better work toward balance?" She almost shouted at me, "I have nothing I can drop right now at all! Monday is baseball, Tuesday is ballet, Wednesday is karate, Thursday is AWANA, Friday is piano lessons, Saturday is Girl Scouts, and Sunday is soccer meet." She started crying. I said, "Something truly has to give, Loni. Which of these can we cut?" She looked horrified and quickly answered, "No way! This is just how life is. I'm not taking anything away from my kids. I'm a good parent!" Most children's leaders report parents not having money to take vacations and sometimes to pay the light bill. But they are still shelling out more than $500 every semester for soccer. These are truly child-driven homes. Parents are accustomed to having every place they go catering to this child-run lifestyle—the pediatrician's office, pediatric dentists, pediatric podiatrists (fitting children's shoes properly), kids' meals at every restaurant, play areas in the park and the mall, our school systems, and so on. Church is about the only place that parents' high expectations for quality family offerings may *not* be taking place. The culture has changed to become more child centric, but the church, largely, has not. Many churches are still operating in a culture and a system that is long gone. Look at your church. How many young families are you attracting? I am not condoning or applauding a child-run household. In fact, I see a lot of red flags in a lifestyle driven only for the desires and perceived needs of the child. But if we are truly going to reach the young families in our culture, we must, at the very least, understand how they operate and think. What is attracting them to our church, to a better knowledge of Jesus Christ, and what is driving them away? One immediate problem that arises with being stuck in the past is that a church's budget may reflect on old way of thinking: adult ministry first, then teenagers, then just enough to keep children seen but not heard. Parents' priorities are the opposite: the very best for our kids, then ourselves if anything is left. These differing expectations run right into each other. But chances are, your church *does* care about ministry to kids. Most of these budget issues are entirely unintentional. The church may be waiting for a quality ministry to support. So how do you put together that all-important first budget?

DEVELOPING YOUR FIRST KIDS' MINISTRY BUDGET

1. Find out what was spent this year, and then the last five years on children's ministry at your church. Find out why certain years may have had a larger number than others (VBS one year? Large equipment purchase another?) Ask your church for a sample of a well-written budget.

2. Starting with your vision and goals (see why you needed those first?), begin writing down what you will need to make that vision happen. What will you need to hit your goals this year? Be realistic, especially when you are starting out. Don't ask for five thousand new chairs the first year, when you are currently running fifty children. Writing your budget with a balance of faith and wisdom, is difficult, I

know, but you'll get better each time. Perhaps ask for one or two larger equipment items, like a new curriculum or service-planning software, but only if they directly benefit your new vision and direction.

3. Get help from someone who is really good at writing a church budget, preferably someone familiar with your church's budget system. My first year at one church, I got help from a youth pastor who gave me great tips. If writing a budget is not your gifting, don't try it on your own. To grow your credibility with the staff and board, it is imperative that you turn in a quality, well-written budget.

4. Study samples of budgets from other churches and kids' ministries. Yours will not and should not be exactly like theirs, but it can give you ideas and help you remember items to include. Examples: glue, nursery supplies, worship DVDs. It helps to see what others have thought of.

5. Do a full church inventory. I cannot emphasize this step enough. Most churches do not suffer for what they don't have; most pay through the nose because they are unaware of what's in those dusty ministry closets. This is something I always do, and you would be surprised at the things I find. At one church they assured me that they had absolutely *nothing* for children's ministry. No equipment at all. Everything would have to be purchased. I thanked them and decided to do an inventory anyway. In the bottom of one closet I found $2,380

worth of brand new puppets, still in their cases. On a shelf in the barn I found costumes, electronic games, sets, and even a portable stage they had bought eight years before and forgotten about. Get a couple friends, a pad and paper, and explore every nook and cranny of that building. Find out what your kids' ministry already has before buying all new supplies. You may be pleasantly surprised.

(We found these awesome sheep hoods during an inventory)

6. Work your contacts. What are churches near you getting rid of that you need? Can you trade sets with another church? Networking is key to successful ministry. Watch those kids' ministry Facebook and Google groups. I get so many great sets and props and even sound systems for free or at reduced prices. I often trade sets of puppets with another church. It helps us both with our lack of storage issues, while saving us a lot of money. One children's pastor I know heard that an arcade was shutting down in another state. He borrowed a semi trailer

and picked them up for only the cost of the gas. Networking can be that outstanding. With whom can you start networking right now?

7. Get extreme couponing, sort of. Check out www.childrensministrydeals.com, www.kidology.org and other sites like it. You can sign up for free samples of curriculum and so much more. One leader I know got free curriculum she needed; another got deeply discounted worship DVD's. It is worth it to shop around and save money.

8. Learn to love rationale. What is rationale? Budget rationale means logical, detailed reasons for asking for something. You should have detailed rationale in writing for everything you request as well as how it directly ties into the vision of your church and the kids' ministry. Remember, more than likely, the members of your board, finance committee, even other staff may have no idea what "Elevate Curriculum" is, or the difference between a PVC stage versus an aluminum stage. Do not assume that everyone knows what you are talking about. The more you explain, the more detail you can give, the better. Again, if this is not your strong suit, get help.

9. Plan to grow. If your vision is to "win kids and families to Jesus," why does your budget only have enough supplies, curriculum, and snacks for the same eighty kids you had last year? If you really plan to

grow, your budget needs to reflect that. How can you predict how many kids will join your kids' program this year? Well, you cannot predict "exactly." But it says a lot when you put in writing that your area *will* grow. Last year, we decided as a church to go for 18 percent growth in every area across the board. That gave us a goal to aim for and to budget for. Aim high enough to stretch you and your team; but be realistic enough to hit and exceed that goal. That means to add wiggle room to accommodate all those new kids and families who will be joining you by the end of the year! Remember: faith and wisdom.

10. Turn in the budget early. Your budget for the following year should ideally be turned in at least three months before the start of the church's fiscal year. Let your pastor or financial committee know you are turning it in, and be patient. Make sure you include anything they ask for, and keep to any deadlines they give. Remember, this may be new for them too. Have courage and ask for the supplies and ministry equipment you believe you will need. "You have not because you ask not." Most kids' pastors who tell me, "My church will not give to kids' ministry," or "My church doesn't want to help the kids" have never asked. Until you have truly worked on a budget proposal, you cannot truly make any of those statements. Completing the budget is an opportunity for the whole church to work together for great good.

11. Stay accountable. Humility goes a long way. When writing your budget, plan to keep good records, and turn in your receipts. Be prepared to answer any questions that your lead pastor or the board may have. Occasionally I run into a children's leader who has the attitude, "Why should I have to turn in receipts? Why should I have to have any rationale? I'm the leader; they should just trust me. It's a church; not a business. This is about the kids and my vision from God; if they say no then they don't care about kids!" This is an extremely dangerous attitude for any minister. Too many kids' pastors come off with a diva attitude or an emotional martyr meltdown on the budget altar. Here are a few important reminders:

A. Accountability is not only biblical, it protects you. We see in the news that pastors are frequently accused of financial impropriety. Even if you're pure as the driven snow and never tempted to impropriety with money, all it takes is one accusation to tarnish your career, potentially forever. Along with a sex scandal, a financial scandal can mar your church's reputation for years to come. Requests for receipts, records, and accountability are not signs of "mistrust." These steps hold all church leaders accountable and rightly so. Help those who are in charge of handling the money, and please do not be a pain in the neck for them. God forbid, if money ever was missing or misallocated, if you ever did get accused, those people, and those records will be a heaven-sent help for you.

B. Everything changes when you realize that the church budget isn't really about money as much as it is about "people's tithe money." God's money must be handled with more care and discretion than any "business." When you think about how some people trusted God, trusted the church, and gave sacrificially, it should be sobering. That is a huge responsibility. Most churches have several ministries to support with a finite amount of money spread across many pieces of the pie.

C. The leadership of any church wants to know that the person leading in any area of the church is responsible, respectful, and mature. This should go without saying, but in all things respecting the church budget be the consummate professional. Church ministry is not just a job. Our heart and emotions are tied up in every part of it. But you cannot ever allow yourself to resort to crying, pouting, gossiping ("can you believe they don't care about the kids?"), yelling, "getting people on your side," or threats (I'm leaving the church!). Unfortunately, I

69

have seen this many times. That behavior accomplishes nothing except hurting the ministry you lead and effectively destroying your credibility. Emotional outbursts cast doubt on your ability to be a strong, effective leader. Do not burn bridges. These are people you will be working with for years to come, God willing. That first budget is a chance to learn and connect, so approach the opportunity with humility, professionalism, and, above all, grace. No diva peacock feathers.

12. Be patient and temper those expectations. Chances are, you are not going to get everything you ask for that first year. If you do, great. Maybe you did not ask quite big enough. But usually, you are going to have to wait on a few things. Children's ministry is about doing the best with what you have and waiting on great things to come next. At the last two churches where I worked, I made them a deal my first year: I will do the best with this budget, but as we grow, excel, and outgrow, I want you to meet me halfway. Each time the churches did just that—waited and watched how things were growing, then expanding the budget as we went along. It's about steadily growing in faithfulness and credibility, and sometimes it's about having to ask again and again.

Remember: it is always a delicate balance. You must balance respect with passion. Many times you will be the only person in the room who knows the needs of the children's department. You are its voice! Make sure that voice is clear, passionate, and direct. Many new children's leaders apologize all the way through their first budget, like they are committing a crime just for asking. Apologizing chips away at your credibility. The kids' ministry is important—to God, to your church, to the parents, the kids, and to you. Ask well, and don't apologize for asking.

For example, as one kids' ministry grew, I knew we were going to have to add a part-time early childhood person. The job had just grown beyond what I could handle by myself. With fear and trembling, I prayerfully wrote up a proposal for an early childhood coordinator. I was so excited for the possibilities and prepared for lively discussion.

They turned it down. They said we hadn't shown we needed one yet. It was "too much money." I thanked them, did my crying at home, squared my shoulders, and dove in to do my best in ministry at the church. I waited six months and then rewrote the proposal, this time with a graph showing how the children's department had grown and a chart of projected growth for the next year. It was the best proposal I had ever written, but they turned it down. So I waited six months and resubmitted it. They turned it down again. I waited another six months, hit total meltdown of stress and exhaustion, and tried again. This time they accepted it, and I got to hire an amazing early childhood leader. We doubled our kids again in only six more months.

I thanked God every day that I didn't burn bridges, and I didn't give up. The new leader was worth every delay. Have patience, and show your work. By the way, God really seems to reward those who are faithful and serve with a great attitude. Still thinking that it is impossible to have an impactful children's ministry with little budget? Consider the words of internationally known children's minister Jerry Moyer of Jubilee Gang Children's Ministry:

> We have noticed everywhere we have gone, in every area of the country, larger churches with terrible children's ministries, awful kids' areas, the worst people over their kids' areas, huge shortages of volunteers, and then these little churches busting out amazing kids' ministries out of nowhere. Why? They have big vision, and they just decide to care. They go after kids with a lot of hard work, creativity and passion. –Jerry Moyer

Rock on Jerry. Let's go after children and families with passion and wisdom. Rock on children's leader. Rock on.

Chapter 4

Choosing a Curriculum

Kerri wadded up another sheet of paper and hurled it toward the waste can, where it landed on a pile of more wadded paper and tumbled onto the floor. In the past four weeks since taking on the kids' ministry at her church, Kerri had thoughts ranging from, "Oh, I got this," "Wait, what is going on in here?" and "Okay, this will work," to "Dear God, I have no idea what to do!" Sometimes she thought all these things in the same hour. Coming up with a vision and goals was more work than she had imagined. Just last week, Pastor Andersen let her know that he was so sorry, but the budget for the next fiscal year was going to be due in less than a month. Writing this budget without a vision or direction just wasn't working at all. What could work in a hurry to fix this mess? She just needed answers and direction. Oh, if only she were going to the big church just a few miles away, the one with a real kids' pastor, the one everyone was whispering about. She had heard rumors of their big kids' musicals, volunteer rallies (they had volunteers?), and their exciting new curriculum.

Wait. Their exciting new curriculum. Kerri's eyes snapped open and her head popped up. That's it—a new curriculum! That could be the answer. Which one did they use again? She picked up the phone and called a friend who had "scoped out the other ministry." After a few minutes talking to her friend (who cannot be named to protect her spy secrets), Kerri became convinced that this was the answer she was looking for! This could save them all.

With a heart full of joy, Kerri ran down to Pastor Andersen's office to tell him the good news. They were saved. All they had to do was order the curriculum! Pastor Andersen listened with great patience, smiled, and said, "That sounds great, Kerri. Can you get me a price quote on that curriculum? And I would really like to know what denomination it comes out of. What are the key competencies that our kids are going to learn?"

Kerri was stunned into silence. Her mind went around in circles. Price? How bad could it be? Curriculum comes out of denominations? I had no idea. What on earth is a "competency?" Instead she sputtered, "Um, sure. I can find that out, like, right away."Pastor Andersen smiled, "Good job, Kerri. It sounds great. Let me know what you find out!"Kerri sprinted back to her office and opened a search engine. She immediately found the miracle curriculum. It looked perfect! Now, where is the price? Oh, wow. That can't be right. No one would pay that for curriculum. There's no way. Then with a shock that she felt down to her toes, she had the sudden realization that the huge price tag wasn't for the curriculum. It was for the activity pack that was sold separately. What? It took the better part of an hour to finally figure out which part was the main curriculum. To her horror she realized that it had to be purchased separately for each age group, and none of the art or activity supplies were included! The media DVD was sold separately too. The final price set her hair on fire. How on earth could she pitch this to her church's budget committee and Pastor Andersen with a straight face? This was more than they paid for their last car. Well, it makes sense to have some back up curriculum right? There must be more out there.

There were more out there. Most were a whole lot more money than she had imagined. Why is this so confusing? Now she was seeing labels for "small-group curriculum" "large group sessions," and "game time." Which one did she need? All of them? None of them? She briefly wondered if she could get samples and try each one out for a month. Then she remembered that several of the teachers complained that the curriculum had changed too often already. They were hoping for stability this time. How could the new curriculum save the kids' ministry, if she couldn't even pick one? Somebody help!

Have you ever felt frustration like this while looking for a curriculum? Finding the right curriculum for your church's vision and culture, that is also right for your group of kids, is crucially important. If you are wondering how and where to start in your programming search, please consider first these common "Myth's of Children's Ministry Curriculum."

Myth #1: Switching to the newest, trendiest curriculum will save our kids' ministry. It will give us a shortcut to the vision and direction we need.

Truth: Curriculum is a great tool to accomplish the goals set by your vision for ministry. Curriculum cannot take the place of a vision for ministry. That would be like borrowing someone else's sermons or vision and thinking it would work exactly the same in your church. In the late 1970s, having a bus ministry was trendy and every church ran out and bought buses. It worked in some and didn't in a lot more. The result? Every church has a broken down bus somewhere on its property. Here is something to remember: Curriculums come and go. There is a new trendy one out at least every other year. I have seen many in the past few years, and churches will get so excited, buy the curriculum, rename their kids' church by that curriculum, get T-shirts with that logo, and paint their walls for that curriculum. But within two years the trendy new curriculum is obsolete, forcing a complete overhaul of the mission, vision, and branding of the department. Overhauling and changing the vision of your kids' church every two years is costly, both in budget dollars and volunteer turnover (many times volunteers that buy in just for that vision will be gone when it changes). A much better idea is to do the hard work; don't skip it and look for shortcuts. Get your vision and mission together for your ministry *first*. That shouldn't be changing every one or two years anyway. Then find the best curriculum to fit your church's mission and values (more on that in a minute). If you need to switch curriculum down the road as one becomes outdated, your branding and mission stay the same; only the means of delivery change. When your dynamite vision and mission pair with a sharp curriculum, you will see momentum. Everyone will feel the direction change; and you will have lasting buy-in from parents and volunteers.

Myth #2: We should try a different curriculum every month till we find one we like.

Truth: Although curriculum doesn't last forever, you still need to treat it like a long-term investment for several reasons

A. It costs quite a bit of money (usually) for a quality curriculum. Constant change costs the church a lot of money.

B. Your volunteers will not like the constant switching. They have full-time jobs that they go to all week; they do not have time to keep relearning a new system. Most volunteers have a "favorite" curriculum. Switch too quickly from their favorite and they will walk. Children's leaders need to be respectful of their volunteers, who are giving up so much of their time to minister to kids. Do not randomly keep switching curriculum without very good reason. And if you have tried fixing the curriculum, working with it, tweaking it (without violating the copyright, of course) and it is just not working anymore, then your job becomes communicate, communicate, communicate. You know it has to be replaced.Find a way, through surveys, online feedback, or volunteer forums, to really take the pulse of your leaders' feelings. What is working for this group of kids? Get their thoughts on the switch, and vision cast. Your ministry will be better off if your leaders are bought in to the vision of your church and your kids' ministry rather than last year's curriculum. Help them see that ministry to the kids and the church is long term and more lasting than any curriculum. You cannot be in every classroom, so listen to those carrying out the curriculum. Don't dictate and shove copies into their hands. Partner with your leaders in creating a kids' program that lasts.

C. Constant change of curriculum wears away at your credibility as a leader. It starts to look like the church cannot figure out which way it wants to go. A children's pastor named Laura started at her first church with a lot of challenges. For one thing, she was the eighth elementary leader in only eight years (red flag). When she went into the supply closet, she was shocked to see at least ten different curriculums laid out, with all their supplies. None of the curriculums were alike, reflecting the fact that each kids' leader took a different direction. When Laura brought the leaders their curriculum for the next week she asked, "So, how would you feel about a change in this curriculum?" It was one she did not care for at all. The first teacher, a twenty-year veteran of children's ministry, responded curtly, "Who cares? I guess I'll teach whatever. It'll change in a week anyway." Most of the other teachers responded in a similar manner. Parents were even more irritated. They never knew what their children would be learning. Every time a parent started to understand how this particular curriculum was working, it changed again. Laura fought the temptation to ignore their frustration and just jump in with changes. Instead she called a volunteer forum and a parent forum to discuss the curriculum issues. She sent home a curriculum survey and then opened up a discussion about it on Facebook. Some of the feedback she received was brutal. Parents and volunteers had no confidence in the children's ministry because of the constant changes. However, many people were shocked that she was actively pursuing their opinions and input. When it came time to start making the changes, she started communicating with leaders, parents, and kids early on, before anything started changing. She assured them that this time, these changes would be for the long haul, because they reflected the mission and direction of the church. When the time came to launch, her leaders were excited and onboard. They gained a lot of new teachers who had been scared to jump in before. And parents were all abuzz wanting to help out. (This is a true story, by the way, and Laura's elementary area of that church tripled in only twelve months.) Stability and intentional direction will gain you loyalty and credibility. You need your team rock solid to see any success or growth in ministry. Let them know that they can count on something.

D. Constant curriculum changes cause a lot of needless repetition of Bible stories and themes. Kids need repetition, but remember, we only have them a limited time every week. We cannot afford to lose time staying on King David for eighteen weeks straight. Too much curriculum switching wastes a lot of time.

Myth #3: The best kids' services are read out of a book. If I deviate from the book, I'm a heretic.

Truth: If all you do is read from a book, you are going to bore the kids right out of church. And that really would be a sin. Without breaking copyright, you should be piecing together a service for your group of kids, never rotely reading to kids. Curriculum is a great place to start. But the more live elements you can add the better. Live, when done with excellence, always trumps a canned offering (see chapter 9), just like fresh hot Chinese food always trumps what's been in that fridge for two days. Live takes time and a lot of hard work. But it is worth the payoff in having an excellent ministry that is relevant to your audience and makes an impact that lasts. Don't just pop in the video and push play and tune out. Craft a service that will reach these kids where they are. Putting together a kids' service is not reading a lesson in algebra; it is setting up a play date with God. Venture "off script." Let creativity and God-ideas flow! I tell my teachers all the time: the child always comes before the curriculum. If a child is hurting—parents going through a divorce, grandma in the hospital sick—take time out to minister to that child. The rest of the curriculum for the day can wait indefinitely.

(Kid's accepting Christ at a midweek Awana service)

Have you wondered: Should we write our own curriculum?

Good question. Some children's leaders attempt this, usually because of the high cost of curriculum. I actually started writing curriculum when I was sixteen years old. I have now written fourteen curricula series and several kids' musicals to go along with the visions and missions of churches where I've worked. I have also used a lot of prepackaged curriculums over the years. So here is what I can tell you about the pros and cons of writing your own curriculum:

Pros: A. Writing you own can be the best way to offer a unique, cutting-edge service. If you have a writing gift, and perhaps a great team, you can tailor-make an amazing service to your particular group of kids. I highly recommend working with a team of creative individuals to craft services that are the gold standard of excellence. Most of the largest churches end up going this route because the expectations for megachurches are so high, and no curriculum out there can measure up to that. All of the largest churches I know are producing their own curriculum, and many of them offer it to other churches. I do not recommend writing your own just to save money. It's not about CHEAP. If you choose to write your own, it needs to be because you feel led by God to aim higher in creativity and excellence, and you are willing to put in the work.

B. You can do more than one series that mirrors what the lead pastor is doing. It creates such momentum when the people of a church can all move in one direction together. Parents and kids all talk about the same message as they go home from church. There is power in that.

C. You can make sure that the kids get everything your church or denomination believes in. It will exactly match your vision and goals. And just like the main service, you can pray about your message, and get something new and real from God for your kids right where they are.

Cons:

The cons of writing your own curriculum for kids' church flow from the next myth.

Myth #5: Writing my own curriculum is just easier than buying one.

Truth: Actually, the exact opposite is true. It takes just as much work to put a kids' service together from scratch as it does to put together the main service, if not more (if you are going with a live band, a drama and dance teams, etc.).

Con A: This is going to cost you a lot more time and will require writing skills. Not many people have the writing talent needed, or the time to commit to putting the services together.

Con B: You cannot do it yourself. You will need a team of people with the right skill sets to make the services a reality. Besides writers, you'll need sound and AV people, gifted musicians, artists for sets, costumes, puppeteers, and actors. I cannot emphasize how huge an endeavor it is to write a curriculum. I personally have found the payoff to be worth the price, but I wouldn't recommend writing it if this is your first year.

Con C: You will spend a lot more time researching competencies, scope, and sequence. Most lead pastors rightly ask the question, How do we know that all the Bible stories and themes will be covered? (Scope and sequence.) How do we know that our children will get everything they need to learn? (Competencies.) And this is the same question that parents should be asking too. Those who decide to write their own need to sit down and write (two years out at least) which themes and stories they are going to cover and when. Please seek input from your senior leader on this too. Those writing their own have a lot more work and preplanning to do.

Con D: If you do not work with a great team, when you end up leaving, more than likely the curriculum will end with you. That will mean on top of you leaving, and a new leader coming on, they will need to switch curriculum too. That's a lot of change.

So pray about writing your own. It's a huge decision and not to be made lightly. I currently use a prepackaged curriculum for the summer, so our team can spend the summer writing our curriculum and service plans for the next school year.

Myth #4: There are a lot of curriculums out there and they are pretty much the same.

Truth: Relatively speaking, there are not a whole lot of kids' church curriculums out there. Not a single one can be everything to everyone. Several I have ordered turned out to be weak on biblical teaching. Some try so hard to be nondenominational that they do not say a whole lot of anything. Do your homework and learn which denomination produced your curriculum. Does it fit with the vision and values of your church? Curriculums vary in content, length of time to prepare, small group and large group formats, and being book or media driven. Doing your homework is essential. Getting a sample of the curriculum to look at first is also a good idea. And be careful: cheaper is not always better. I've seen great curriculums for all different prices. Price should not be one of your criteria for introducing children to Jesus, His way and His words (the Bible). I would look for *correct*, *current*, and perhaps *comprehensive*, but not *cheap*. If you get a great deal or are able to make a trade with another children's pastor, that's wonderful. But choose it because it is the right fit for your vision and your church, not because it was cheap. Our kids need us to make the investment in their lives and their eternity.

Pastor Trisha's pet peeve #2168: Why do we spend hundreds if not thousands of dollars on our kids' sports, music, and education without batting an eyelash because it's "for the kids"? But when it comes to our children's knowledge of God, His Word, and their all-important spiritual formation, we don't have the money and have to look for "cheap"? Do we pick their bicycle helmet because it is cheap? When my daughter needed a pediatric surgeon, I certainly did not search under "cheapest." When searching for the right curriculum, look for the best quality and the right fit, not the cheapest.

The following true story from a lead pastor is one I find very frightening. It is something to keep in mind when picking your own curriculum:

I have been a senior pastor for 22 years now, and 6 years ago, when I first took my current pastorate, I started right away setting up youth and kids' ministry. We had trouble finding anyone to take on the kids' ministry, so when we finally found a young lady willing to do it, I was elated. She seemed to be doing a good job at recruiting, setting up classrooms, getting a puppet ministry going. I told her we would need to order more curriculum soon, because we would be running out of what I had ordered a few months before. (I did all the ordering myself back in those days.) She said, no problem. A week later she told me she had found an amazing deal on curriculum and saved us an unbelievable amount of money. It just seemed too good to be true. I was asked her how she managed that. She told me the name of the curriculum, and I had never heard of it. I thought it was something new that had just come out. I asked how the leaders liked it. She said they were going to love it because it was so much less work. I had a nagging feeling that I should dig deeper, but I had so many other things pressing on me that day. So I promised myself that I would ask more questions later. As the "nature of the beast" goes, I got distracted with several other areas and all the ministries we were launching at that time. About a month after my initial conversation with my children's leader, I just happened to be walking the church and praying one day when I passed one of the primary children's classrooms. I stopped when I didn't recognize the book on the table. Out of random curiosity I walked into the classroom and picked up the book. I thought, "Ah, this must be the new curriculum we ordered at such an amazing price! I hope it's as good as she says." As I opened the book and began to look through it, right away my stomach sank into my shoes. In cartoon form and clever object lessons, this book laid out "Bible stories" and "Bible lessons" that would never be taught in any evangelical church I know. Most of this went completely against everything our church taught and believed. This sounded alarmingly just like something I had just taught in a Wednesday night class about the occult. Feeling like I was going to throw up I flipped the book over to see who published it. Sure enough, the same cult group I had just been "decoding" last Wednesday night was providing the systematic teachings given to the children of our church every Sunday! I literally ran classroom to classroom gathering up all the "curriculum" books, and I called a rather panicked meeting with my children's leader. She was mortified and upset. She had no idea who had published the book. Even when I told her, she had no idea who that group was. She had just loved the full color pictures and art ideas, and the fact that it was so little cost to the church. The whole incident shook us up. It did not save us money because I had to throw out all of those books and start from the beginning purchasing a new curriculum. But now we check, every time, before we buy. This could have been a lot worse, so we are a lot more careful now."

—Pastor Ryan

You've got me convinced, Pastor Ryan. Let's check out our curriculum thoroughly before we buy!

With all this to think about, how do you choose and implement the right curriculum for your kids' ministry? Here are the steps:

1. Always start with your church's and kids' ministry vision, mission, and goals in mind. Match up a curriculum that fits with your church's culture and needs. Not the other way around.

2. Obtain samples and price quotes for several different curriculums for consideration. Write out the pros and cons of each.

3. Find out the denominational background of the curriculum. Determine its scope, sequence, and proficiencies. Do they fit your vision for ministry? To what extent does this curriculum use actual Scripture? (this is important- some use little or none, concentrating on "good character traits) etc.

4. Identify the needs of your unique group of children. Children are all unique, and no group of kids are alike. This goes along with knowing your audience. What challenges, joys, and fears are these children experiencing right now? Does the curriculum you are considering address any of these? Does the curriculum give them the tools and point them to the One Who can help them through what they will face, now and in the years to come?

5. Have you chosen to have your children's ministry be small group— that is, Sunday school classroom style? Or large group—stage, kids' church, all-in-one-room style? Or do you do plan to do a split of both?

Each church has its own philosophy on this matter, some with very heated debate! The decision affects everything from the layout of the space (one large room, many classrooms, or both), to the curriculum, recruiting, and the use of the illustrative methods. I personally like for the kids' ministry to reflect the philosophy of the church as a whole. Most churches advocate that their parishioners attend one large worship service each week, as well as a small group during the week to make friends, connect, and learn deeper doctrine. This is a healthy model for children's ministry as well. Children need to be in a large group service to learn how to worship in a corporate setting, to give to missions, to learn to pray together and for each other, and to connect to the church as a whole. Large group is the best place for them to learn to serve and be a part of the illustrative methods such as dance, media, and drama. Small group is a great place for kids to make good Christian friends their own age, connect with Christian leaders and mentors, and learn the deeper biblical truths. So if you ask me which curriculum you should use, large or small group, I answer yes. BOTH. And I like curriculums in which both large and small group portions flow together.

6. Talk to other kids' pastors and leaders in your networking groups (you have been networking right?) about which curriculums they have

used. See if there is a church that will trade curriculums with you. Sometimes you can both benefit from a trade.

If at all possible, make a trip to a church using the curriculum and watch it in action. Nothing works better. Gather those leaders and make a fieldtrip!

7. Keep your leaders in the loop with forums and feedback forms. Give them a chance to weigh in and gain their support.

8. Keep your parents and the church at large in the loop: communicate, communicate, communicate. Take the time to set things up with excellence and earn credibility.

9. Find out if there are conferences or trainings for your intended curriculum. Some I have used offered free training or sent a representative to our church. Others have had pricier trainings, but they were well worth it. Take as many of your team to these trainings as you can.

10. Don't forget to add up the entire cost. Does your curriculum of choice recommend certain worship music or a DVD? If so, are they sold separately? Are set plans or other materials included? One curriculum we purchased didn't seem to be so costly at first, until we realized that we needed a lot of supplies set up in every classroom each

week. The cost of the extra supplies was a lot more than we had bargained for.

11. What is the human cost? How many hours of set up are involved, and who is going to do it? How much set up is required of your volunteers? Please be considerate of your volunteers' time. Remember how valuable they are to the ministry and that they work regular jobs during the week. Curriculums are vastly different in how much set up they require. Some have little to no set up (a few copies, a few markers, etc.). Others are time intensive (4 pink ping pong balls per room, one hairdryer per room, seven music posters per room, 14 purple crayons, etc.) I picked an "awesome, cutting-edge" curriculum once, without checking on the amount of set up. Our poor administrative assistant and summer intern spent hours and hours just on the first week packing up bins of cotton balls of certain colors, balloons, water colors etc. for each room. They may still not be speaking to me. I told them if they do not forgive me, they cannot get into heaven. It's in the Bible. I've read it. But I will not make that mistake again. Some churches have knowingly picked a curriculum with a lot of weekly setup and intentionally assigned someone to do it right from the start. It works better if you plan for the amount of set up from day one and have a backup if the regular person gets sick! Make sure little to none of that

set up ever falls on your regular teachers; it needs to be ready when they come in.

This goes double for portable churches. I have attended and helped with several portable-church ministries. One common mistake that is made early on in is that someone picks a trendy new curriculum, or one that is working great at one campus, and implements it at the portable church with much-less desirable results. Why? Portable churches have a unique set of advantages, including visibility, appeal to the unchurched, excitement, and momentum. But a good kids' leader at a portable church also is aware of its unique set of challenges, not the least of which is the complete set up and tear down every week. Usually, a portable church must have an amazing team of people to come in very early every Sunday to set up everything: chairs, sound system, walls, screens, instruments, and so on. This puts serious time crunches on that team, and everyone works hard and fast. So imagine how much these time problems are compounded if you choose a curriculum requiring hours of additional set up? Make sure you do your homework and choose a curriculum you and your leaders can realistically do every week with excellence. Tips for portable church curriculum set up: (1) Choose one you can really live with. (2) Clearly assign someone to prepare during the week and set up on the day of the class, and have a backup. (3). Pack bins during the week with everything prepared for each classroom ready to just open and go. Pack up your bins early in the week and double check them Saturday for accuracy. (4) Do your copies in bulk. Most portable churches do not have a copier, so try to copy your curriculum months or quarters at a time.

Note: Curriculums come and go, Scripture does not. Don't die on the altar to any curriculum. Hopefully, the curriculum you pick serves your church well for a long time. When it has run its course -just the curriculum, not your vision or mission- have the courage to let it go and begin the process of selecting a new curriculum.How do you know if a curriculum has truly run its course and needs to be replaced? Curriculums are long-term commitments. Hopefully you don't need to change them all that often. But wait too long and it can do a lot of damage. Here are some signs that your current curriculum may be getting outdated or be in need of a change:

1. It is a remnant of a vision or mission for the church that no longer exists. It served someone else's vision long ago, and the vision it supported is no longer the vision of your church. For example, years ago your church was doing "the purpose driven church," and the kids' church changed curriculum to "the purpose driven kids' church." Now

your church has changed its mission to "reaching our world, one relationship at a time." But the kids' church is still using the same purpose driven curriculum. The rest of the church is going a new way; the kids' ministry was left dangling. Time for a change.

2. The kids are no longer getting the jokes or references. Everything is so outdated that the kids cannot relate or connect with what is being taught.

3. The teachers do not want to teach it. They are not excited about it. They make excuses not to show up. You know for a fact that several of them are just teaching their own thing because they despise the curriculum that much. Time to amputate (the lessons, not the leaders).

4. The kids don't want to hear it. They are bored, acting out, disengaged. They are not excited to be there. They are making excuses to not show up. They are not inviting their friends.

5. The parents don't want to hear about it. They aren't showing up for parent meetings, and they don't want to sign up to help. They are bored and checked out and making excuses not to show up. Stop blaming parents and kids for checking out. Blame won't get it done. Time to give them something they can't wait to show up for.

6. It no longer fits your format. For example, if you were once all small groups (Sunday School) and are now switching to a large group (children's church) format, this will necessitate a curriculum change. New vision, new direction, new format is a great time for a new curriculum.

Keep praying throughout this whole process, and you will see: a curriculum change for the right reasons, implemented the right way, with the right planning can ignite your kids' ministry service to a whole new level. Use with caution; this kids' service is now power packed and extremely contagious!

Kids will *want* to bring their friends, and their friends will want to bring their friends. Can you see all those kids excited and ready to hear about Jesus? Oh yeah, we are going to need a lot more help.

Chapter 5 Recruiting Part 1

Strategies That Fail or "Throwing Up Your Bat Signal"

It's no secret that I love a great superhero movie. Day-to-day life, especially when you are serving people in ministry, is plenty real enough for me. I'm not a fan of "reality" TV. So when I sit down to a movie, with my popcorn and Sour Patch Kids, I want a happy ending. You know what I mean: superheroes showing up right on time, annihilating any challenges. Super flight! Laser eyes! And don't you just live for the part, right when all seems lost, all hope gone, the commissioner is ready to turn off the signal, hang up that desperate call for help, at that last moment—the hero shows up and swoops in to save the day. You want to stand up and cheer. Good wins. We are a part of that big win, part of the team!

I have yet to watch a superhero movie about a commissioner sitting up late on a Saturday night making tired, desperate phone calls:

Yes, Mr. Crimson Flip-Flops, I know it's not really "your calling," but we need you! Didn't you see the hopeless signal? The lost-cause beacon? The city is going to burn to the ground soon anyway, but wow, we could sure slow it down a day or two if you would help. No one will help, and I mean *no one*. Rattail? Yes, Yes I did call him. He's got a "thing" he forgot to do. Mullet Man? Well, he just hasn't had much time to get "fed" lately, so he's taking some Mullet Man time. Dame Scare Hair called in sick—a week and a half ago. Yeah, a little suspicious, I know. And the rest didn't call me back. Look, I've been down the whole list and really, it's a very short list, and well, you're our last resort. Come on, fill in just this once? Otherwise, we have to close the city down. You heard me. Shut the whole city down. Think how much faster it will burn down, then! I just wish someone would want to help! Why am I the only one in the world who cares? It's okay if you are terrible at fighting fires. It at least looks better if you are here, and we won't have to close the city. Any superhero will do. Or any person, dressed convincingly in a costume. Or a mannequin in a towel. I mean, sometimes we gotta take what we can get, ya know? What? No, I'm not crying. Why would you think that? You think I'm some kinda failure? I'm not, okay? I'm sorry. I'm sorry okay? I just gotta fill this opening. Oh, thank God. Whew. No, no worries. No, you don't need to prep. Just show up tomorrow morning, and we will hold on a little while longer. Oh, thank goodness I can go to bed now. Night. Oh, how I dread doing this again next week."

That would make a terrible movie, and no one would ever sit through it. Yet I just described a few of the most utilized kids' ministry recruiting techniques out there right now (guilting, pleading, settling, under asking, under expecting etc.) We've all made those calls, including me. But those late-Saturday-night calls need to be a last resort, after all other recruiting strategies are in play.

"How can we recruit help?!" is the number one question I am asked over and over by churches large and small all over the country. And I am about to lay out a few techniques that I and other children's pastors use with success.

But first a word to all of you who, in desperation, skipped the first four chapters and came straight here for a quick fix for your scheduling holes, I'm not judging you. Okay, maybe a little. But you need to understand. There are no quick fixes to recruiting, training, and managing volunteers. As those  who read chapter 2 know, (you guys get a gold star), all recruiting flows out of vision. Anyone you recruit to "fill a spot," "kick off a curriculum," or "help me out for a couple weeks" is *not* going to stay. The recruitment techniques I'm going to share with you are designed to flow out of prayer, planning, and preparation to ask quality people to partner with you in a strategically designed, high impact ministry. No shortcuts are here; the volunteers you may find with shortcuts will do just that: shortly cut and run.

If you remember "survival-mode" from chapter 2, it is the position from which too many children's leaders recruit: guilting, pleading, stalling for more time (to do what? Survive?). Throw survival-mode out the window. Do you want them to serve in the children's ministry? Tell them *why*—why it is a win for them and the ministry. Grab that vision you developed in chapter 2; that is your call for recruitment.

Let's look at the common mistakes that just about every childrens' ministry leader makes at some time or another:

Mistaken Play #1. The Sinking Ship

Premise: Scream that the ship is sinking and everyone will climb on board. "We need some help or we will have to close the nursery! No one is showing up, and we have a lot of holes."

Why it doesn't work: What do rats do on a sinking ship? They trample each other to run away. No one wants to feel like it is all on them to "save" anything. Especially not a volunteer who has another life the rest of the week. People quickly sense when there is no direction, no plan, and no one at the helm, and they quickly run away from serving in that area. Remember: no vision, no plan, means no volunteers.

Once I visited a church plant that was just getting its kids ministry off the ground. The church as a whole was growing fast and was already standing room only. They had more than enough greeters (the greeters have awesome matching vests and "big" jobs to do during the service) and plenty of set-up and take-down people. You could tell the volunteers were excited; they came early and stayed late. They were all smiling and kept asking to take on more. But what the pastor and kids' leader couldn't understand was why they had such huge shortages in the kids' area. Why didn't anyone want to volunteer in there? While I was sitting in the congregation, the pastor said this from the pulpit: "Just wanna thank all of our amazing set-up and take-down people, our greeter team. I appreciate you all so very much! We are changing the world for Jesus! Oh, and um, my wife told me to say that we need a few people in the little kids' area, and, just talk to my wife about that. The kids are out there (pointing to the kids' area). We really need somebody in there, and I'm sure she has the details on that."

This is what the congregation heard: "I, the pastor, so appreciate the greeter and set up teams. You mean so much to me. What you are doing is important. We are a part of a winning team. Our vision is to change the world for Jesus, and we are winning at our goal. On a side note, my wife is making me read this, that we need somebody to babysit other people's kids somewhere over there for free. I'm not sure where, or any of the details, but it is not important to me, or to the vision of the church. And it's not going well, because no one wants to do it. Someone join the team that is losing, so that this team can go on winning. Someone go fix that little problem, so that the rest of us can get back to our mission and vision here."That, of course, is not what the

104

pastor said, but it's what I believe the congregation heard. Not surprisingly, *no one* signed up (or talked to the pastor's wife) to volunteer in kids' ministry, but he did gain twelve more greeters and six more set-up people. Now, it would be wrong for the children's leader to say in frustration, "See! I knew it. No one cares about the kids. I'm the only one here that cares about the kids." That would not be true. The problem here is one of vision and communication, and it *can* be corrected. (I'll show you a better appeal in the recruiting techniques chapter.)

Mistaken Play #2. The One-Hit Wonder

Premise: Thinking that one massive recruitment campaign, one pulpit push, one co-op is going to "fix" the staffing "problem" forever.

Why it doesn't work: This may be the most depressing paragraph in this entire book. There is no "one thing" that will "fix" your recruitment needs forever. Recruiting new leaders is integral to your role as a children's leader. You will *always* be recruiting new people. Always. And you should always have spots to fill. Why? Because in the natural course of life, people move away, they transition to a new position within the church, God calls them to a different church (yeah, I just said that), people die (yup, just said that too), and as your ministry expands and grows, you should always need new people to grow with it.

Anything living grows, and you need new leaders always flowing in to meet that growth.

Do not fall into the trap of thinking, "If we were a megachurch, we would never be short of people again." I'm laughing right now, and so are all my staff, because even at one of the largest churches in the state of Ohio, staffing is always one of our greatest challenges—and one we make happen with the grace of God! With that many leaders on any given weekend, someone (usually more than one) will always be sick, out of town, or have car trouble. The truth is you will always be recruiting. You'll just get better and better at it!

Mistaken Play #3: The Never-Ending Apology

Premise: Constantly apologizing for asking people to serve in the kids' ministry.

Why it doesn't work: Please, please. Just stop it.

A recent article I read stated that women are four times more likely than a man to apologize all the way through a presentation.[8] Those constant apologies foster distrust in listeners, causing them to be much less likely to approve whatever she is proposing. The more I

---

[8] Brian Williams, NBC Reports, *Sorry, it's true, women apologize more.* http://www.nbcnews.com/id/39384763/ns/health-womens_health/t/sorry-study-shows-why-women-apologize-more/#.VAOcfMVdWro, 2012, accessed May 2014

thought about this article, the more I believed it. But I have heard both female and male children's leaders apologize all the way through their appeals more times than I can count. When I tell them, "Hey, here is what you said," they sputter, "Me? No, I *never* apologize when asking for volunteers." So now I usually record it and play it back for them just to show them how many times they actually do it. One young lady apologized nineteen times (I counted) in a ninety-second appeal asking people to serve. So she apologized roughly once every four to five seconds. That's a record, so far.

Before you start yelling that you would never do that, I challenge you to record and listen to yourself when you do an appeal. Also read your email and voicemail appeals. Did you know there are a lot of ways to say "I'm sorry" without realizing it? How about this children's pastor's appeal, with my thoughts in parentheses:

Hi, I'm Pastor _____. (So far so good.) Can I have a minute of your time? (Uh oh. Said every vacuum salesman/Jehovah Witness.) Sorry (1), I don't do this very often (Why tell them this?) So excuse my (2) nervousness. This Scripture (read verse) oops (3) lost my place, sorry (4). What I need to tell you is this: I'm no expert (5). (If you are up there talking about it, we all consider you the expert until you told us otherwise. Why did you just tell us this?) But I really think (You think or you know?) we need people badly in the preschool area, because we have a lot of holes. (Why do people not want to work there?) We are just doing our best over there, and we need you. (Um, you want me to do better than you at it?) So if you could just spare a little of your time, just an hour a month, (Wow, you really do not expect much.) please, we could really use you. I'm never too good at this (6). (At what? What exactly are you asking me to do? How do I get started?) So I hope you'll bear with me (7). (You are up there and I don't have a choice.) So if you can help, let me know. (How can I let you know? Where do I find you? What are the steps? What exactly do I have to do? How can I get my questions answered? Oh never mind.) Thank you for giving me your time. (This can count as another apology, such as, Sorry I took your time.")

Contrast that with a different children pastor's appeal I heard about a year ago:

Hey, I'm _____, elementary director here at _____, behind me you'll see pictures of the elementary dance team doing ministry downtown for our Love

Your Community Day. (Whoa, that is amazing.) Our kids'
ministry is growing *fast*! (Something cool is going on there.)
Our mission is to reach the kids of this city with the love of
Jesus, while meeting their needs in a real way. (They know
what they are doing!) I want to take this moment to thank our
leaders for making this happen! You represented Jesus well
that day, and what a difference we made! (These leaders are
valued, and they are winning at their mission, a mission that is
important!) With our classes growing this fast, we are going to
need a more people on our team, so I am taking applications
for our next season of programming. (People *want* to do this.
They don't just take any trained monkey.) Are you interested
in more information on joining our kids' ministry team? (Yes,
I'd love to be a part of something like that!) It is *not* easy, and
sometimes it breaks your heart. Like last week, when six-year-
old Hannah from the homeless shelter walked barefoot to the
parking lot where we were ministering because she wanted to
hear the music about Jesus. She hadn't had a meal in a day and
a half. We fed her a great meal, prayed with her, and she won
a teddy bear at the end of the day. I'm telling you, the cost is
worth the difference we get to make in kids' lives and in our
city! (Oh, my gosh. I'm crying.) Don't wait. (I won't!) Sign up

today. (Where? How?) For more info call us at
_____ email us at
_____, or you can find me immediately
after the service at _____.

She had me in tears, ready to sign up right then! It's no
surprise that she had a flood of
signups—and a lot more growth over
that next year. What did she do right
with her appeal? She pushed vision,
strategy, and excellence. The ministry
was winning at a goal and the
volunteers were appreciated. Long-
time international speaker and
children's pastor John Tasch teaches
the difference between a help-wanted sign, which says to people, "We
are understaffed and you will probably have a long wait and poor
service," and a sign that says "Now hiring," implying "Wow, this place
is growing and people are applying to work here!" See the difference?

There is one overarching reason to never apologize for asking someone
to work in children's ministry:

SERVING JESUS AND HIS KIDS IS THE GREATEST
OPPORTUNITY SOMEONE CAN BE A PART OF.

Being a part of explaining the story of Jesus to a child; being
there when they "get it"; praying with them to receive salvation; seeing
them learn to talk to and experience God themselves; helping them find
their God-given gifts and the joy of serving—these are the greatest
moments I have ever had. Offering someone a chance to use their gifts
for something that matters and will last into eternity is the kindest thing
you can do for them. You need to understand this down to your soul
right now.

If you do not see the "mission critical" impact of what you do,
no one else will either. If you don't believe in the eternal significance
of what you are doing, right down to your toes, how can you ask others
to take on this journey with you?

You see, American culture has it all wrong by supposing that
volunteering is a nice thing to do if you have extra time. Scripture tells
us that every Christian—not just the pastor—is to be actively engaged
in serving and using his or her gifts to serve Christ, His church, and the
lost. Our consumer mentality tells us that the church is here to serve
and entertain us by providing us with something. This thinking couldn't
be more wrong and unbiblical. In reality, God created and loves His

111

church desperately. The church is a hospital, a rescue center, reaching out to those without Jesus, and training and equipping Christians to reach the lost. We are to train Christians how to serve to their fullest potential. This serving is not optional; Scripture warns that God will hold us accountable for how we use our time, treasure, and talent. On that day, when everyone gives an account for how they spent their lives, when only what was done for Jesus matters, how many will be ecstatic that you asked them to serve? So do not hesitate to give someone the chance to serve—and do not apologize for doing so.

Mistaken Play #4: Barring Men from Serving in Kids' Ministry

And now an important word about men and children's ministry: In my humble, yet totally correct, opinion, we need to stop barring men from our children's ministries. I have seen this trend at some churches lately. The reason, when you boil it down, is this: people fear that men working with children may secretly be pedophiles and that parents will be afraid to leave their children with a man in a classroom, especially in early childhood. News stories of late have only added fuel to this mania. In response, some churches have removed all men from their kids' areas and even refuse to recruit men in kids' ministry. I would laugh at this if it weren't so very tragic. The second church where I was on staff had this rule, and we were desperate for leaders in the kids' area. To my horror, I found out the church did not even conduct background checks on the women who served because "women aren't pedophiles." Wrong! Women can be pedophiles, and the number of women sex offenders, though still far behind men, is rising.[9] I demanded that all women in our kids' areas undergo a background check, and I received heavy sighs and eye rolling. One administrative assistant finally said, "What for? They are women!" We all were unprepared, however, when the checks revealed that *two* women applicants for key teachers in the preschool area had felony convictions for child molestation. One had even lost custody of her own children. We never would have known that if we hadn't checked. I changed the whole way we recruited and thought about our kids' ministry that day. Everyone underwent a background check. And I opened the door for men to serve in the kids' ministry again. Some men were hesitant to sign up, however, because they didn't want to be viewed as a potential child molester.

Do we understand how biblically far off we are when we do this? Where does this thinking come from? Actually, the way we think of kids' ministry as a whole isn't biblical at all. In Deuteronomy, God commands the whole congregation, especially the men, who ruled that

---

[9] *Why Female Sex Offender Numbers Are on the Rise,* article by Elev8 News, March 9, 2012, accessed March 2014
http://elev8.com/569555/why-female-sex-offenders-numbers-are-on-the-rise/

patriarchal society) to make sure that the next generation would know God and His Word. Nowhere in the entire Bible is the spiritual formation of children written off as "women's work." Spiritual training was the job of the father and mother of the home and ultimately of the entire congregation. In fact, Jewish boys by the age of five were instructed by skilled teachers of the law—all men. Part of what happened in our early American culture is that children were viewed as inferior and unimportant, and carted off to another room to be "babysat" while the important adults had church. That posed a problem: who is the least important person we can spare to go babysit while we have church? Usually it was the young unmarried girls.

The Bible tells us clearly in both testaments that God cares dearly about the next generation. He directly holds His congregation responsible for these young ones, to make sure that they know HIM and His Word. He doesn't take it lightly when this teaching hurts His kids (think "millstones," see Matthew 18:6). The church should never allow cultural pressure or the latest headlines to scare us into operating any ministry in an unbiblical manner. Right now, more than 53 percent of the kids in my congregation are in single-parents homes. Many of these homes are run by a single mom. So many kids have no father figure at all. Almost all of their public school teachers are women also. Many kids are desperate for a strong male role model to show them how a man of God acts. Not a perfect guy, just a man who loves Jesus!

So what happened when we started recruiting men and allowing them to serve in kids' ministry? Panic and mayhem? Not at all. Amazingness is what happened. We gained some of the best leaders I have ever known—strong men of God who have prayed for, been there for, and lovingly taught these kids. Right now almost 61 percent of my kids' ministry volunteer force are men, and I haven't had any parent complaints. We were ready to address any concerns, but we decided to completely get behind our volunteers and unashamedly begin promoting this more biblical view of kids' ministry. We put all of our leaders in the classroom because they are well screened, and we believe in their ability to serve our kids and church well.

I thank God for all of our volunteers—men, women, teenagers, grandparents. We know that reaching our kids for Jesus is the job of the congregation, not just a few women between the ages of eighteen and fifty. Even though my husband and I have a great marriage, I am so grateful for the Christian men who have taken the time to set an example for my son and for my daughter. It was one of these dedicated teachers, a grandfather, who led my son to Christ one Wednesday night—and it brings tears to my eyes even as I write this. If you're having trouble getting enough people serving in kids' ministry, for heaven's sake, and the kids' sake, don't tie either of your hands behind your back.

Mistaken Play #5: Limiting Students from Leading

It took me a few years to develop my current philosophy of youth ministering in kids' ministry. It all started with me getting my start in kids' ministry at age 14 with a pastor who took a chance on me, giving me the training I needed. I have always wanted to pay it forward. At each church where I have been on staff, I get better at putting together groups of teenagers who lead dance teams, acting teams, sound and lighting teams, and more. Everything came to a head for me when my assistant kids' pastor was diagnosed with cancer. In only 11 weeks, Sonya, age 34, was gone. I was devastated and ill prepared to fill the gaping hole she left behind. To my surprise, one 14-year-old girl stepped up to lead the worship team "in the interim" for us. She grew so much, she just stayed at it for several years. It ended up that the worship team became so much bigger and more effective than I could ever dream; they opened many camps and events in our state. Also during that interim, a 12-year-old boy began stepping up more in the sound and lighting area. By age 16 he was our kids' ministry intern and took over the leadership of the kids' worship center media team. One very special 13-year-old girl started taking on more and more of the choreography of the dance team and writing of drama material. Five years later I hired her full time as assistant children's pastor. She is currently a gifted and passionate kids' pastor and worship leader at a church of her own.

As the team of teenagers kept growing, I thought, "Lord, where are all the adults to do these things?" I felt God answering, "I'm not afraid to use young people, so why are you? Let them lead."

So I did. I devoted myself to mentoring this young growing team and letting them have more and more creative control. I remember one particular Saturday-night service, I finished prepping the team, rehearsing the latest dance number, then promptly went into the bathroom and started vomiting. The stomach flu had hit me out of nowhere, and I couldn't get off the cold clammy bathroom floor. One of the team came to check on me in the bathroom; she was scared, but she knew, ministry has to go on. So she went back in the kids' worship center and directed all the teams. I heard that the service that night was amazing—without me. I was so proud, and I began to realize something I had not noticed before. These wonderful kids sitting out there in the seats every weekend did not want to be a 30 year old with two small kids. They didn't want to be *me*. They desperately, more than anything, want to be teenagers. Talk to these kids like a kid, and they tune you out. They want to drive, date, dress, and dance like a teenager. Look at any kids' show on Disney or Nickelodeon. Those are not kids or adults in those shows. Those are teenagers who sing, dance, and act. The secular world has tapped into something significant. These kids are hardwired to follow what their older counterparts are doing. Just watch. Whatever the teenagers are singing this week, the kids will be singing next week on Kidzbop 214. Whatever the student ministries girls are wearing today, your kids' church girls will be wearing tomorrow (yikes). It does not matter at all if these young people *want* to be heroes or role models. They already are. Scary as that can be, isn't it smart and strategic to intentionally create role models whom you want your kids following? Give them some heroes worth following. And that means doing whatever it takes to have a great relationship with the youth pastor and a presence in the student ministries. You are not in competition! You are complementing each other's ministries.

Earlier I quoted some very scary statistics stating that we are losing the majority of our Christian kids before the age of 18 (they leave church and most do not come back). There is a lot of debate about why that is, but here's what I have concluded: We lose our young people because we do not include them. In the book <u>Artificial Maturity</u>

by the brilliant Dr. Tim Elmore, he points out that we are overstressing, yet under challenging our kids. (He mentions that less than one hundred years ago, teenagers were leading armies!) I feel it is tragic not to engage our students in servant leadership. Why in the church do we babysit these young leaders, wanting them to "sit down and be quiet" while the adults do "big church." Why are we so shocked when they turn 18 and find the church completely irrelevant to their lives? We never taught them how to use their gifts for God. We never engaged them. It was never *their* church. What a waste. It is time and talent we will likely never get back. Where else in the church can young people have so many opportunities to minister than in the kids' ministry? Drama, dance, speaking, worship leading, tech, classroom help, and more. Every time I have a teenager speaking or leading worship, they have the full attention of every child in that room. The kids are glued on this "rock star teenager" who descended from on high to speak to them. That's a big responsibility; and I have my youth teams sign conduct forms as well. I expect a lot from my teenage help, but I give a lot in mentoring them too. I feel so strongly on this topic, I turned down working at a church that had a policy against students serving in ministry. Take a chance. Reach out and engage the next generation in ministry. Most churches have a policy that there must be at least one adult per room, but these teenagers can still be amazing leaders.

Challenge them. They will often do the crazy things your adults leaders refuse to do (dunk tank into green Jell-o, human burritos, green ape outfits) If God is not afraid to use young people, you shouldn't be either. Go open the door for those young people to serve. Don't let anyone close it.

I asked Becky Goerling, a 16-year-old kids' church leader from Ohio, what she would say to a brand new children's ministry leader. Here is what she emailed me in response:

What would I say to a new ministry leader? Hmm…Don't ever give up, not on yourself, not on your ministry, and not on your kids. When someone says patience is a virtue, they mean it. Working with kids takes time and effort, and it's totally worth it to build relationships with the kids. Keep teaching, so they have excellent examples of God's love and compassion. I'm just a regular high school teenager, nothing spectacular, no degree or training. I just wandered in one day and loved it. I kept going back and kept getting more involved.

I believe children are better examples of Christ than adults could ever hope to be. These kids have shown me a hope and perseverance that I will never forget. Like during our latest musical outreach we did, my grandmother had passed away the evening before. But I just couldn't stand to let those kids down—could've called my understudy, could've just sat out. But I was there during practice, I saw how hard these kids worked, I saw how much heart and soul they put into this. I saw elementary school kids who worked harder than some adults. I dare anyone to challenge the power kids hold in their hands and in their minds. Children can soften the hardest of hearts and bring grown men to tears. They are phenomenal. I love kids' ministry. Every second I've spent with these kids I wouldn't trade for anything in the world. –Becky Goerling

Mistaken Play #6: Lowered Expectations and Teeny-Tiny Asks—The Truth About UnderAsking.

Oh, I know, you are thinking, "But I'm constantly asking!" I'm not referring to how often you ask, I'm referring to how *big* you ask. Most children's leaders under ask. It comes from that age-old survival mentality we discussed. This starts with an appeal fraught with loads of apologizing. The thinking usually goes something like this: "Wow we are so desperate, and maybe we would get a lot more help if we ask as little from people as possible! Let's make the work seem so easy, with no prep, as if anyone can do it. We just need a warm body in there, or we gotta close the class. It's so simple that it's trivial. Just take your turn and get through it!"

Besides reeking of babysitting and desperation, the mistake of under asking chases off great leaders for this reason: time. Have you ever noticed that despite our many modern conveniences, faster modes of communication and transportation, thousands of labor- and time-saving devices we are busier and more stressed than ever? Studies show that people today have actually have *more* leisure time now than they did forty years ago.[10] So why are people busier and more stressed than ever before? They are driving their kids to soccer, ballet, and speech meets, working a lot more hours to make ends meet, and then volunteering at their kids' schools. These people are tired.

So why is it a mistake to downplay what you are asking them to do? To make it sound as small and easy as possible? Because people

---

[10] Elizabeth Dunn and Michael Norton, CNN Special, June 21, 2013, *You have More Time Than You Think,* posted http://www.cnn.com/2013/06/21/opinion/dunn-norton-time-famine/, accessed April 2014

"How We Spend Our Leisure Time," by Po Bronson (2006). *Time*

"Americans Have More Leisure Time Than Ever," by James Joyner (2006). *Outside the Beltway.* www.outsidethebeltway.com/americans_have_more_leisure_time_than_ever/

are constantly bombarded with opportunities and demands to work or serve, but most of them are a blur of things that nearly anyone could do. People get really tired of being guilted into all of those areas too. Trust me, people! I've done the 1:00 a.m. baking of three dozen cupcakes that my child told me about that evening so that I am not the "bad parent" who wouldn't help with the fourth-grade bake sale. But in this world where people have limited time to give, we still have a longing to be part of something meaningful that will live on when we are gone. We want to use the gifts with which God uniquely created us. We want to be a part of something amazing. We want the sacrifice of the time we gave to matter.

Even with being so busy, volunteerism in the United States has never been higher.[11] But people are not going to give a moment of that precious time to something that anyone could do by just showing up. We want to be where we are needed and can make a difference, where our skills and gifts play an integral part on a winning team. No one is going to deliberately sign up for the team that just announced it is losing. That investment of time must go where it will bring the greatest return. The surprise for me in my many ministries has been that I find more gifted invested leaders when I ask *big*. I ask and expect a

---

[11] Corporation for National and Community Service Statistics Corporation for National and Community Service Statistics, 2009, http://www.nationalservice.gov/impact-our-nation/research-and-reports/volunteering-america

lot, and that attracts people who want their gift of time to matter. For example, we once asked for people to help in a classroom once a month for a two-month commitment with no set-up or extra work required. We had almost no takers. Then that same month, I made a push for fine arts team leaders. I made it clear they would have to be there almost every Saturday for two hours rehearsing, live up to a strict code of conduct, come prepared to lead devotions and pray together, and learn to lead the younger leaders. I had so many responses that I had to rotate teams and make a waiting list. I am not promising you that same result. What I am saying is this: when the need is big, you may need to ask bigger. How important is kids' ministry to you and the future of your church? How about to God? So much is riding on the next generation and their relationship with Jesus Christ. Don't the kids deserve a bigger ask? Think of the United States Marine Corps' new slogan, "We except commitments, not applications."

Need proof? How about the most amazing ministry recruiter of all time—Jesus. How did he go about recruiting a team to launch His brand spankin' new church?

First He prayed. A lot. Sometimes He spent all night praying. Before you say that sounds cliché, have you really spent quality time in prayer asking God to give you the right people in the right positions?

Second, Jesus asked big. He said, "Leave everything—your job, your family, your house, your money, and come follow me right now." And they did. They must have sensed His authority and His vision, and they felt called to Him and His ministry. Later He kept saying things like, "I am going to die for this new church, and most of you are going to die for this cause too." WOAH. Not the pep talk we are used to getting!

Third, Jesus never apologized or begged anyone to come onboard. Show me the verse where He guilted someone into "just filling that spot for a couple weeks till we can figure things out." Didn't happen! How can you come closer to Jesus' way of recruiting? Pray, ask, and leave behind all apologizing, begging and guilting.

Here are a few more tips for asking bigger and better:

1. Don't say "anyone can do it." No one is going to sign on as a "warm body" for a position that even a monkey or a warm mannequin can do. People are looking for something that will challenge them, use their skills, and make a difference for eternity.

2. Don't minimize the importance of what you are asking them to do. No job serving Jesus and His kids is unimportant.

One wise children's pastor decided to change the way that volunteers looked at serving in the nursery. He said, "We will no longer advertise for 'just caring people to hold babies." He instituted a simple curriculum for the nursery, the first of its kind. Then he announced that every baby would be introduced to worship songs, every baby would begin to learn a Bible verse, and most importantly, every baby would be held and prayed for each and every Sunday service because he wanted every child in his ministry to feel the love and presence of God, to know the joy of singing praise, to start early loving God's Word. WOW!

This of course, added a lot of new duties and much more commitment to the nursery leaders. As you probably guessed, his leaders loved it. They finally felt that the ministry they had been doing was valued and meant something. All of the sudden he had people signing up left and right. Not because it was the easiest or had the "least prep." They signed up because they wanted each of those precious babies to know the love of God from day one. Every area of children's ministry matters. We should never undersell the work involved.

3. Don't say, "minimal commitment." Ask volunteers to commit (usually a written commitment works best). How long should you ask your leaders to volunteer for? Well, usually forever is too long. Don't leave the commitment open ended. Have a time limit in case the volunteer is not a correct fit for kids' ministry. Most churches go with either a nine-month (school year) or one-year commitment. I've seen a lot of elementary and pre-K ministries use a school-year commitment and nursery to age three ministries use a one-year commitment (the children are not in school yet).

4. Hold a high standard. Include with your commitment form a code of conduct that matches your church's vision and mission. Be specific and put in writing what you want them to do. For example:

• Arrive twenty minutes early.

• Participate in a volunteer opening prayer rally right when you arrive.

- Be prepared to open the doors promptly at ten a.m.

Let volunteers know in writing that they may be asked to step down if they are found in breach of that commitment. Find out what gifts and talents they bring to the table and incorporate those giftings into that class schedule! Got a puppeteer who signed up to help in the 4k classroom? Get him (and his puppet) telling that story ASAP. Each leader should be fully invested in the ministry. People who find their place to serve stay. Floating people leave. We have a big job. Let's get them to it! Ask them to be a part of a team. Ask them for their time, talents, and heart. Ask them to partner with you in reaching lost people for Jesus!

Now you know what doesn't work. What can you do to get those volunteers you so desperately need?

Chapter 6

Recruiting, Part 2

Techniques of Wonder and Awesomeness

The question most kids' leaders ask at this point is, "Which recruiting strategy do you recommend for our church?" And my answer to that is … "Yes." By that I mean, you will probably need to engage your church with several if not all of these strategies at one time or another. The reason is that the people in your church all have different learning styles and ways they like to be asked. Studies now show that due to the constant barrage of information being shoved at us on a daily basis (marketing noise), most Americans need to hear or see something seven times before it actually sinks in! Yikes! And sometimes we need to see it in several different forms. So, don't be afraid to over communicate your vision and your call for leaders in as many forms and in as many ways as possible. Feel free to get creative and try ones not listed here (Gasp!).

Recruitment Techniques of Wonder and Awesomeness

Recruitment Technique #1: The Pulpit Appeal—This occurs when the lead pastor or the children's leader appeals directly to the congregation from the stage during a weekend service asking for volunteers. What could possibly go wrong?

Pros: The pulpit appeal is the gold standard in children's ministry recruiting. Some of you may be asking, You mean there are other methods? Yes, but we will get to those in a minute. Why can it be a win? When done well, you have the ability to impact a larger number of your parishioners at one time with your appeal. The superintendent for my district once said, "Visibility lends credibility." Go memorize that now. Back already? The main win from a pulpit appeal, if done well and especially if your senior leader does it, is that it shouts to the entire body like a bull horn: "OUR CHURCH VALUES CHILDREN

AND FAMILIES. WE VALUE THIS MINISTRY. IT IS PART OF OUR VISION AND MISSION. IT IS IMPORTANT AND YOU SHOULD BE A PART OF IT." Every childrens' pastor needs this kind of backing to see some mountains move. In a day and age when some churches are making the decision to not do any pulpit pushes anymore, I still can see the value in showing your whole church that the kids' ministry is there and growing. You have to remember, most people sitting in the adult service have no idea what is going on in that other room. Out of sight, out of mind. And if something is stuffed to some far-off room, how important can it be? If, as the kids' leader, you have any opportunity at all to speak to the congregation as a whole about the kids' ministry, take it. Go speak for those kids, those volunteers, and for the parents. Speak well and gain church-wide credibility for a ministry that is a part of your church. Let them know the kids' ministry is not just child care in a far-off room. Be clear about the successes. Indicate where anyone can get more information about coming aboard (not a sinking ship, but your totally tricked-out semi nuclear bat-hover yacht, patent pending). Rehearse what you are going to say in front of a mirror over and over until you've got it right. It also helps to get some feedback from a friend before going on. (I do this all the time).

Cons: You didn't know there were cons? Well actually the pulpit appeal has a lot of cons, and a lot of room for a belly flop. And that is why many churches are moving away from them. Where do I begin?

A. *Attractin' the crazies.* Okay, that was way too harsh. Maybe. But the major drawback to the pulpit appeal is that you typically get a lot of signups from people who should not work with children. Also, most high-quality leaders will not respond to an open "cattle call." That is not universally true; I have picked up some amazing leaders from pulpit appeals. But I have also had sign ups from people who were legally restricted from having anything to do with children, people who had been asked to leave the children's ministry years ago, people with anger-management issues, people who hated children, or people who just signed up for everything. And I think you know what I mean when I say some people are just not a fit for children's ministry. This problem is made much worse if the pulpit appeal was done incorrectly. If someone pleaded and begged from the stage saying, "We are desperate. We just need anyone. It's so easy anyone can do it. Just sign up and we'll get you in there," now you really have a problem. You may have to tell someone who signed up, "We are desperate, for anyone at all, anyone can do this job—but we do not want *you.*" That gets personal and hurtful. And it typically makes the church look heartless and hypocritical. Do not fall into this trap. You can avoid it by not doing pulpit appeals. But let's not throw the baby out with the bath water. You can avoid some of this embarrassment by doing the appeal correctly. Be honest with people! The ministry is for children, and you cannot take everyone. Everyone in the church can and should find a place to serve, but not everyone can serve in children's ministry. You are going to find people who are a right fit for children's ministry. Do your background checks; some will be weeded out right away. Some churches require references from the last place the volunteer served, which can help weed out a few more. Ask other staff and key volunteers about the history of a person at that church. Above all, trust your gut. If you just don't "feel a peace" about putting someone in a children's class, please listen to that warning. It has served me well. You do not have to be insulting, but that person can probably find another place of ministry in the church. Your priority here is the safety and well-being of the kids.

B. *Dropping the ball on follow-up.* One pitfall of the pulpit appeal is when your team fails at follow-up. The pulpit appeal is a great way to get a lot of names of people wanting to learn more about serving. But each and every one of those names must be contacted, sometimes more than once (or four times). It is a mistake to simply expect that all of those people are now "committed," then to celebrate, thinking they are all showing up to help on Sunday. The sad fact is that when it is all said and done, only about one-quarter of the people who sign up for a pulpit appeal will actually work out as viable children's ministry volunteers. Some will never call you back. Some went home and changed their mind. Some sign up for everything and are too embarrassed to tell you they are overcommitted. Some will be disqualified due to something in their past (child-abuse conviction) or in their present (alcohol addiction). Some will come the first day and then not show the next. So why do this recruiting thing at all? (Insert yell of frustration and throwing hands up in the air in despair here.) We recruit because that 25 percent of people who sign up and do become great leaders are worth the work involved to bring them onboard. Keep going after these people; they are like gold when you do find them.

I need to say again that it's critical to call (and get hold of) each and every one who signs up. And do not assume that "someone" will take care of it. It is too important to assume anything. Weeks before your pulpit push, assign the person who will call these people, and set a deadline for the calls. I set aside the week after a pulpit appeal and clear my schedule just to call all the people who responded and follow up on those who are hard to reach. Why is follow-up so very important after a pulpit push? Because several churches reported making the decision to discontinue pulpit appeals entirely because more than one person complains, "I signed up, but no one contacted me. I guess they just didn't want me. I guess they really didn't need people that badly." But I hear children's leaders say, "Well, we were getting to it, but we got so busy." You are so busy because you need that volunteer help. If you aren't going to call every single one, do not ask for signups. Then you can have fun continuing to do it all yourself. Getting the help you need is work, but so worth it.

No matter what the reason, if people are signing up and they are not getting a call back, it looks bad. It looks bad for you, for the church and for the kids' area. You look disorganized, ungrateful, and unprofessional. It discredits you, and hinders any future recruitment. I spoke with an amazing volunteer a few weeks ago, a pediatric nurse with years of experience in children's ministry. Out of curiosity I asked her, "Mary, why didn't I get you back here helping me sooner? You are amazing!"

She answered, "Because five years ago under a different pastor I signed up to help in kids' ministry after a pulpit appeal and no one ever called me. I even called to ask about it, and no one called me back. I was so hurt that I did not ever sign up to volunteer again. I felt like they lied from the stage by saying, 'We are badly in need of help.' And I did not want to be a part of anything so disorganized anyway. If they cared so little for people that they can't make a phone call, how are they treating their volunteers?"

Mary really made me think, and you should be thinking right now too. Your word needs to mean something. If you say from the pulpit that you will follow up on the people who sign up, then come what may you had better make good on your word.

A good rule of thumb is to aim to make initial contact with everyone who signed up in the first week after the pulpit appeal. Call in help if need be to make those calls. If a parent or volunteer calls you, return that call within twenty-four hours. No excuses. You need that help in your ministry? Don't want to keep making those Saturday-night calls? Then this work has to be done. No kids' ministry can run without great volunteers; so use this opportunity to treat them right from the outset!

C. *But what about the other departments?* Usually when a church is moving away from pulpit appeals, this excuse (con) is raised. It typically goes like this: "If we let you make an appeal for leaders in kids' ministry, to be fair we have to let every area of our church—all 347 of them—make an appeal, and we will never have another church service again! It will just be nonstop begging for helpers!" My response has always been to quote Andy Stanley, "Who says we have to be fair?" No, you do not have to let every single area have equal time from the pulpit. Why does the kids' ministry sometimes need that extra bump? Well, for starters, the kids' ministry needs more volunteers than just about any other area in the entire church. Everywhere I have been, the kids' area has held more than half of the church's volunteer base. The ratios of adults to children that need to be maintained mean that more leaders are required. Since these are our kids we are talking about, not just anyone will be able to serve there. We need the best, highest-caliber leaders with our kids (parents should all agree here too). A good rule of thumb is that a healthy kids' ministry of any church should make up about 25 percent of the church as a whole, plus parents, and volunteers, which means anything you say from the pulpit about the kids' ministry already affects about 60 percent of your church. Kids' ministry is an all-church endeavor. It has to be. Kids' ministry has never been nor can it ever be self-sustaining. Yet it is one of the only ministries in the church that meets during the main service, off in its own area, where many have no idea what is going on in there. Shouldn't the right hand know what the left is doing? Asking the kids' ministry leaders to recruit that many quality leaders with no representation in the main church body is like telling them to double their brick quota with no straw. Studies show that the majority of families are choosing their churches based predominately by what is offered for their kids. The recruiting of these leaders is absolutely mission-critical for the church as a whole. Lead pastors of fast-growing churches know this and make sure to give that kids' ministry a visible, credible shot in the arm every chance they get.

Recruitment Technique #2: The Parent/Grandparent/Guardian Ask— This recruitment push usually centers around calling the parents, grandparents, and guardians of every child in your ministry and asking them to be on the rotation for teaching or helping in their child's class. Usually the pitch goes like this:

> Hey, if every parent took a turn, we would have helpers to spare, and no one would need to be in there much. No one would get burned out! Parents are really the spiritual leaders of their kids anyway (true), so you need to get in here and be a part of what your child is learning. (Also true).

This method stops short of being a co-op because you are "strongly suggesting" and "asking/expecting" all to "take a turn." You really do not enforce this at all. What happens is you need to build a database of all children who attend your church over a three-month period, even if they are only there once a month. Do not include visitors yet, though you need to establish at what point to add them. Once you decide to ask for parent, grandparent, or guardian involvement, advertise it in as many ways as possible. Put it in writing that this is now the expectation. You are going to have to call each and every one and ask them to commit to a weekend or service.

Pros:

A. Getting parents to be more of a part of what their kids are learning and doing! This is a chance to equip parents to be the key spiritual leaders in their child's life.

B. Another great opportunity here is to reach out to non-Christian parents. Several of the parents we asked to help out actually came to faith in Christ for the first time just hearing the simple message of salvation during their child's class! One of my best key leaders came in this way. I don't ever use pre-Christians for lead teachers, but they can make great helpers, set-up people, and more.

C. Parents can reinforce at home what they helped teach on the weekend.

D. These parent helpers have come in very handy for me on days when a regular teacher or helper called in sick or had an emergency. It was great to have the parent standing by as a fill in.

Cons:

A. Parent rebellion. You really need to have the lead pastor on your side before trying to implement this style of recruiting. You will get these excuses:

- "I just can't. I need a break. I have them all week."

- "I used to teach kids' church. I did my time. (Like it's prison) It's someone else's turn."

- "We serve somewhere else"

- "I don't like kids. Not even my own (get that one a lot)."

- "We are so busy, we have no idea when we will be here."

- "We only go to church when the baby lets us, and we have no idea when that will be."

- "I homeschool. Sunday is my day off."

- "My child does horribly if I am in there. Cries the whole time." (Have the parent serve in a different class.)

- "We are overcommitted at school, sports, voice lessons, etc."

- "We serve at a different church. We go to this one for fun."

- "I heard that _____ aren't serving. Why do I have to? Doesn't seem fair to me."

Bottom line: you will have parents simply refuse to take their turn, or they will sign up and then not show up. Some will complain to the pastor that you asked. You will have to be prepared for that. The unfortunate fact is that you cannot count on the parent helpers to always be there. You still have to schedule a regular teacher and helper, and then the parent helpers are a great addition to the service. If you count on them and they do not show, the whole class suffers. So you need to ask yourself, What is my backup plan? You really only have one option for enforcement: moving to the co-op system (discussed below). Just make sure you understand all the pros and cons of the co-op before you make that decision.

B. Not every parent should be working with kids. Yes, I just said that. Not every parent should be a parent. There are parents who have child-abuse convictions, so you still need to do background checks. If a parent is just not a good fit with kids' ministry, for the good of the rest of the kids, please do not put them on the rotation. Then be prepared for other parents to yell, "No fair. How come they don't have to do this?" You will not be able to give them an answer because of confidentiality. You have to tell complaining parents who are serving on the rotation "I cannot answer for another family's situation, but thank you for doing what is right."

C. Not every parent has gifts for teaching or children's ministry. You are still going to need kids' ministry teachers who are *called* and have a gift for presenting the gospel. If a parent is on the rotation but is not a teacher, he or she can still be a great helper, classroom set-up person, tech person, snack person, and so on. *Parent* does not always equal skilled *teacher* or *leader*. The heart and core of a great children's ministry is still leaders who are called to serve Jesus and His kids. Some of the best leaders I have served with through the years did not have kids of their own, or their kids were grown.

D. You are still trying to "force" people who may not want to be there to "take a turn," like this is a chore. This may go directly against your vision and mission, and it begins to smack of babysitting. I always want people serving in kids' ministry who want to be there, who are having fun, and who are making it fun for the kids! I always want people serving alongside me who are there to impact lives for eternity. People who feel guilted into "doing their duty" may come in with bad attitudes, like "let's get my turn over with." Is your ministry something amazing that people want to be a part of, or something you have to force on them? Usually churches resort to this, or the co-op, in desperation, saying "Take your turn with your kid or we are gonna have to close the class!" Many parents, not yet aware that they are supposed to be the number one spiritual leaders in their child's life, may just be "church shopping" for what serves them best. If they feel they are being coerced into taking a turn babysitting other people's kids, they will rebel or find another church. So do you still ask? Yes. I still do the parent/grandparent/guardian ask. I let them know we expect them to take a turn on the rotation. Our serving expectation is written in our new family registration forms, and I always ask them to serve with a lot of vision casting and excitement, never with guilt. I think of these parents as wonderful additions to a great program who may even become regulars. Bottom line: your best leaders must still be skilled teachers called to serve in the kids' ministry. You really hope that some of those will be the parents of these kids. Remember to be patient with parents. A lot parents are in need of ministry themselves. They may be hurting, in crisis, or needing to mature in their own personal faith. The ministry you do with their kids is family ministry as well. Keep that door open and your hand extended, and in time they may be lifting up the arms of that kids' ministry with you.

Recruitment Technique #3: The Strategic Personal Ask—This is the most effective yet surprisingly least used of all recruitment tactics. The personal ask is simply looking with a strategic eye at your congregation and asking, "In my wildest dreams, who would be amazing to have working in our kids' ministry?" Usually these folks are already very busy because they are gifted, smart, and good at time management. They have already served quite a while in the church. They do things with excellence and draw others like a magnet at their "regular" jobs, humanitarian efforts, school board, neighborhood parties, and more. These are what we call high-capacity leaders. These are the people you need to grow your kids' ministry. But they do not typically respond to cattle calls. This is a source of frustration for pastors everywhere. You do 459-plus pulpit appeals for help, then you finally get up the guts to ask this person face to face, and they smile and answer, "Oh, I would love to. I was hurt that you never asked me." AHHHHH!

Pros: The personal ask is many times more effective than any other method at recruiting leaders, especially "high-capacity" leaders, if done well. You target the people you want, do your background and reference checks, and then ask them well. This is one of the only methods you should use for recruiting those key positions, the ones you are going to need as you grow. Remember how Jesus had several tiers to his leadership design? Three were at the top (Peter, James and John), then the twelve disciples, then the seventy, then the multitudes that followed. There were things that Jesus entrusted to only the twelve that He did not say to the seventy. One of the hardest things to do as a children's head leader is to learn how to communicate well with large numbers of volunteers, leaders, parents (the chapter on communication skills follows this one). Even right now, you are going to have to realize that the ministry can never grow beyond you—beyond your capacity to raise up more leaders, beyond your own ability to let go, and your capacity to delegate. As you grow, you must learn to put quality leaders in key positions, such as over Wednesday nights, volunteer training, second-service nursery, and so on. Remember, you cannot find these people from a pulpit appeal alone. These key people are going to come by way of personal requests and interviews. Gaining these volunteers will cost you a lot more of your time. So get asking, and ask big. There is power in boldly asking someone to partner with you in a big mission. The best way to have amazing high-quality leaders is to have an amazing high-quality program. Great leaders will not "fill a spot" or "babysit." They follow great vision. So if you've worked on that vision and mission, it may be time to get asking face to face. Need a first-service nursery worker? Pray about it, then target that perfect person, and go ask them. If she (or he) says no, accept it graciously and go ask another person. Need a Wednesday-night game director? Pray, think it over, then go sit down with your perfect game director and ask. Tell that person why he or she is perfect for this position, has the needed skills, and say exactly what you need. Do not downplay the importance of the ministry or the hard work involved. Look that person in the eye and ask. And if he or she says no, take it graciously, but leave the door open for a change of mind. I cannot tell you how many people have come back later (sometimes more than a year later) to say, "I'm ready now. Throw me in." Pray, hunt, ask.

Cons: A. Rejection. Some people are getting hives right now reading this. The thought of walking up to people and asking them to help you with something is terrifying. What if they say no? What if they are irritated with me? What if it makes it awkward between us? The best way to avoid all the negatives is by asking well. No begging, no whining, and no guilting. You are not trying to sell them Avon or a Kirby vacuum or hand them Watchtower pamphlets. Start right away with vision. What amazing things are happening in that kids' area? What is God doing in there? What is the mission and where is the kids' church headed with it? Ask them to pitch in with their gifts and strengths. Some people will still say no, and that is okay. Do not apologize for asking or for being passionate about the ministry that God has you in. When you start begging and apologizing and guilting, that is where the awkwardness sets in. That is when people will cringe when they see you coming because you make them feel guilty and sorry for you. Instead, give them the opportunity to be a part of something bigger than you, something that God is doing. Expect to be told no sometimes. It's not personal, you didn't fail. The worse they can say is NO, and even then, you have opened their eyes to what is going on in the children's ministry. Keep praying for God to call people and keep asking.

B. Being ill-prepared when someone says yes. What will you do when someone says yes or wants more information? High-capacity leaders will have a lot of questions, and they expect you to have answers for them. How often do you want me to serve (weekly, monthly, bi monthly)? Will I still get to attend a service? What are the steps I need to take to commit and be trained? What training is involved? What will be my time commitment now and after I am fully trained? How long am I committing for? (Don't say life.) What will I be expected to do? Do you have a written list of requirements and expectations or a job description? (You should have that to hand to them.) Answer all questions fully and do not dodge any or make up answers. Sharp, quality leaders can spot a fake. If you do not know the answer to a question, say, "I do not know. Let me get your phone number and email, and I will get back to you on that right away." Then make sure you do. The real con of the personal ask happens when the children's leader has no idea what to say when someone says yes. You can avoid this by having those answers to who, what, when, where, how, and sometimes why. Be prepared for a yes. I have been shocked speechless by some of the amazing people who have looked across the table and said, "Sure. I'd love to get involved. What do I need to do?" I never would have had the highest caliber leaders on my team if I hadn't mustered up the courage to ask.

Recruitment technique #4: The Ministry Fair—The ministry fair is an event put on at your church before and after services in which each area of the church sets up a booth in a public area and elicits signups of volunteers.

Pros: The ministry fair is a great way to put the emphasis on serving church-wide. You are saying, "Everyone in this church can and should find a place to serve." Churches with strong emphasis on serving grow much faster than churches that do not preach, encourage, and foster it. Churches that equip the congregation to use their gifts in serving make a lasting impact on their community and the world. Isn't that what Christ has called us to do? What is more American than a ministry fair? Parishioners walk through a whole litany of booths and choose where they might like to work. You have a great opportunity to showcase all the wonderful things going on in the kids' area. Take that opportunity. Here are some suggestions for a successful ministry fair booth:

A. Bright colored table cloths, balloons (helium), streamers, and so forth. No bare tables allowed. Children's ministry is not lame, and your table can't be either.

B. Lights: colored, spinning, flashing. Perhaps a disco ball, or a fogger. No, I'm not kidding. I use them at mine every year

C. Live ministry: kids in full-body costumes, puppets, singing, and costume characters

D. Video of the very best in your kids' ministry. Show them what they could be a part of!

E. Big full-color pictures of the ministry. Please take the time to do this and every part of the booth well and with excellence.

F. Food: candy, cookies, popcorn, and cotton candy. As petty as this sounds, it's a proven fact that the booth with the best goodies gets the most interest and the most signups. Bribery? Perhaps. But I always get a lot of signups; let's put it that way.

G. Something interactive, like a game such as guess how many of these in the jar.

One big plus here is you may get the opportunity to talk to a few interested folks as they sign up and a get a feel for their level of interest, experience, and gifts. I always go out from behind the booth, talk to people walking by, and invite them to look over our opportunities. Interact with people. Talk to them.

Cons: Just like the pulpit appeal, you will have a lot of signups from people who cannot or should not work in kids' ministry. You should not imply in any way that every signup guarantees a place in the ministry. You will have a lot of weeding to do to find viable candidates. Every signup will still need a call back within a week, so clear that schedule and prepare to contact everyone.

Another drawback is that you are catering to the American "fast-food" thinking that the church is just here to serve its members instead of promoting the scriptural teaching of people using their gifts to serve others.

A third drawback is that if you throw the fair together, or it is unkept, boring, and outdated, you will do more damage to your recruiting efforts than if you did nothing at all. No one wants to be a part of something that is not put together well. Make it excellent so it stands out in a good way.

The fourth drawback is most important: while the fair is underway, the booth must be occupied at all times by a vibrant, happy person. Any booth without a person in it will not get signups. If you are not going to have someone there, do not bother putting up your booth. If you are not going to put the time into it to make it excellent—a representation of your ministry—do not bother having it at all. Do it well and get those signups.

Recruitment Technique #5: Media—Bulletins, websites, flyers. Remember that I said that people have all different learning styles and need to hear and see information many different times in many different ways for that information to stick? In this day and age, communicating effectively through media isn't optional anymore. Gone are the days of handing out a sloppy two-color flyer and expecting results. Just like the ministry fair, it's better to do nothing at all than to hand out something outdated, sloppy, or thrown together to represent your kids' ministry! But never before have you had so many amazing and cost-effective options right at your fingertips. Again, if you are struggling for ideas and expertise in this area, don't be afraid to search for help in your church, from parents, or perhaps networking with another church. Check out what options may exist online (I really like www.overnightprints.com—sharp, well done, and cost effective). Here are a few media ideas for you. But please keep in mind that media is a tool to convey vision. Always include a lot of vision. Media always works best in conjunction with other ideas mentioned here. Now let's delve into some options—and remember, creativity is king here!

A. Website—Make sure you do this right and well. You may also want to open a Facebook for your kids' ministry. Just be careful, that if you do start a website, Facebook page, or other social media site for your ministry that you put in the work regularly to update it. I post updates once a week, letting parents know what is going on. The biggest complaint about ministry websites is, "They never update them. There is no new information. The events are from last year, and the pictures are two years old!" So parents, volunteers, and potential volunteers will stop looking if you fail to keep fresh updates coming. When I do a recruitment push (usually twice a year) I post a video to the website detailing the vision and the steps to serving. These have been very successful and well received. I also have parents or volunteers post recruitment videos and testimonies. Making and posting these videos is easier than ever. I've done some with my smart phone and used editing software on my tablet. Make sure you have signed consent forms from parents, before posting any pictures or videos of minors.

B. Handouts—I am not talking about boring, outdated stuff here. Get creative! One of the best I have seen was by a church that gave out a different handout every week for four weeks. The first week's handout had full-color pictures of famous people—respected politicians, world leaders, humanitarians, scientists, and also several notorious figures from history who people know and despise. The caption read, "Who influenced these people when they were children? Who will our kids become? Who is influencing our kids? Be a life changer. Be an influencer." Included were all the steps to signing up for more information on serving in the kids' ministry. Did you catch the vision and inspiration there? The creativity impressed me and others too. This church had a flood of great signups. Week two they gave out a special bookmark with the best pictures from that year of the kids' ministry. On the bookmark was a reminder for the entire congregation to pray daily for what God was doing in the kids' ministry. Stellar. Think vision; think creatively.

C. The church bulletin—Yes, I know no one reads the bulletin. But cover your bases anyway. Describe the vision and the steps to serving. Be careful not to beg or promise anyone a place in kids' ministry. Your bulletin insert can do double duty too if your church posts the bulletin on its website.

D. Video announcements—This is in effect, a short commercial for your kid's ministry. A lot of churches are switching from pulpit announcements to video announcements, either before or during the service. The main reasons that churches are switching to video appeals rather than pulpit appeals are (1) to control the time the announcements take (live announcements have the potential to go on and on and on and on and); (2) to create and guarantee a higher quality of announcements; (3) to incorporate the announcement video as a creative element that flows with the service instead of breaking the mood with a long litany of announcements that often have nothing to do with the service. If you get a chance to do a video commercial for your kids' ministry, use this opportunity well. It can be a great recruiting tool, that you can use for quite a while, such as on your church's website. Have a key volunteer give his or her best testimony of serving in kids' ministry. Have two puppets argue about who loves kids' ministry more. Make it sharp; creativity is still king.

Recruitment Technique #6: The Co-op—This is similar to the parent/grandparent/guardian ask, only it goes one step further. The co-op system is in use in some churches now, perhaps some near you. If you are considering it, I would strongly suggest you find out how it is working for them. The co-op has the same pros and cons as the "ask" with one large addition: for a child to use the children's ministry at all, usually after a four-week grace period, an adult member of the family must serve in the kids' ministry rotation. You need to thoroughly think through all of its implications before you announce it. The only way to "enforce" a true kids' ministry co-op is to track how many times a child comes and how often the people in the child's house are serving. After the grace period, if no one in that house is serving in kids' ministry, you have to tell the parents they can no longer drop off their child to kids' ministry and that the child has to go with them into the adult service until they are willing to "take a turn." It is typically promoted as "the only way to keep our kids' ministry open," which is a terrible reason. A better reason would be that you are teaching "family ministry" church-wide and are using the co-op to better train parents to be the spiritual leaders in their home. A word of caution if you are considering the co-op: your lead or campus pastor had better be 100 percent behind it before you proceed. And there are several steps that you will need to take before and during your launch to create a successful co-op ministry for your church. Here is a list of warnings and tips to consider before deciding to proceed with a co-op:

A. First of all, when you start turning children, preschoolers, babies away and they start sitting in the adult service, that can be irritating and distracting for some pastors, and they will want to talk to you about it. One pastor I worked for asked us to implement the co-op because he didn't want any more ministry fairs. He changed his mind the very first week that we turned several families with babies back into the main sanctuary. (They refused to use the cry room.) He was so flustered at the noise and distraction and told us never again!

B. There will be parent anger, and you have to be prepared to deal with it in love. Imagine a mom with four small kids (one nursery age). Her husband is deployed in the military. She hasn't made it to church in three weeks. She finally staggers up to the check-in twenty-two minutes late for service but feeling like an exhausted, triumphant warrior just for making it. She missed most of worship, but this will be her first sermon and "break" of any kind in weeks. Then she is told she will have to take all four kids with her into service because she is not "serving in kids' ministry." She stammers that she helped with the food pantry stocking (two months ago). What will she do? Take them to service with her? Go to the cry room (probably to cry herself)? Leave? Right or wrong there's gonna be anger, and somebody's gonna hear about it. Phone calls, personal meetings—it will happen, just be prepared. Most parents will skip you all together and go straight to the lead pastor or the board. You have to listen and respond in love. It's better that they talk to the church leadership than everyone else in the church and community (which is probably happening too, so watch how you react). This is why having your lead pastor's 100 percent support when you start this is so crucial.

C. Decide ahead of time which exceptions, if any, are going to be made. What about staff kids (if the spouses refuse to take a turn serving)? How do you put them back in the service if the parent is on the stage? What about board members' kids? I personally feel that you need to vision cast this and have the rest of the staff and leadership onboard before it starts. You will need the staff and board setting the example, not constantly wanting exceptions. Caution: keep making too many exceptions, and your co-op cannot work. Word will get out and no one is going to "take their turn." What about people serving every week in another area of the church? We wrote in our co-op rules that you needed to be serving regularly *somewhere* in the church, and we strongly suggested the kids' ministry area. That helped us, because some parents were so committed to the worship team or other teams and would have resented having to quit. I don't want resentful people working with our kids. Also, it stopped the question, "How come they don't have to serve and I do?" Everyone is expected to serve on a regular rotation somewhere. What do you do when you have a family that just experienced a tragic loss? Or a family going through a divorce? I think most people in the church should understand that some families need to be ministered to and have ample time to grieve. Two families we have in our church have more than four special needs kids each, and due to caring for their youngest ones they cannot serve in kids' ministry. Again, the church should understand and try to help. In some situations, you just have to use your head, and err of the side of grace. Never forget that this is still a church.

D. You will have to reinforce that you still need nonparent teachers and leaders. Don't let them feel like they are unwanted and unneeded in a "parent-led co-op." Like I said, many of my best leaders, teachers through the years did not have kids of their own. Keep letting those nonparent leaders know you still need them.

E. Your pastor is going to need to give you a lot of "cover" from the stage. You are really going to need him or her to vision cast family ministry co-op from the pulpit. Again, that's why you need them 100 percent with you on this. No vision = no cooperation.

F. This needs to be communicated in every way possible for at least two months before you make the switch: email, flyers, posters, calls, pulpit, smoke signals, flares, fireworks, everything you got. The number one complaint when a co-op is launched is parents saying, "nobody told me." They feel like they had no say and therefore do not need to participate. No matter what, you will still have some who say this, but make sure you did your due diligence anyway.

G. You will need to do the work and prepare ahead of time. Put systems in place before you launch. You need a way to continually track each child's attendance and the parents' involvement in serving. This is important not just when you launch but from here on out. You need to know when a parent is not showing up anymore to take their turn—no call no showing—so you can follow up with them. If they keep not showing up, how many warnings will you give? And you will have to decide at what point the family can no longer use the kids' ministry and let them know. All this tracking and follow-up is time consuming, and it's smart to have your systems in place before you launch. At our church, we use a website—www.fellowshipone.com— for child check-in. But it also has a nice feature that lets us print out child attendance and parent serving records every week. It saves us a lot of time!

H. No matter how well you initiate your co-op, just understand that some people will leave the church. It used to be that your church was just your church for life, no matter what. But these days, with our consumer mentality, too many people are in a church because of what it offers them. As soon as you start expecting something from them, they may just go somewhere easier. Never make your decisions in ministry based on what may make people leave! Make your decisions by what is right. But do not feel surprised or shocked when you turn people's kids away and the family does not come back, no matter how "nicely" it is done.

On a personal note, I'm not a fan of co-ops. I understand the reasoning and I agree with its principles, but it breaks my pastor's heart to look at an excited child who is peering into the kids' church room all raring to go and I have to tell the child that he or she can't come to church today because his or her parents are "not on the list." To be honest with you, I wasn't able to do it. I want kids to want to be at church. I want the child in that service and God wants to connect with him or her. And what's more, I want the child's parents to want to serve in our services. Does it work to force them? I don't know. I've never gotten a committed key leader out of a co-op. I despise the whole idea of forcing people to take their turn. My teams can't wait for that service on Sunday, the kids can't wait, and I never like someone dampening an awesome service with a resentful attitude. Jesus gave us the parable of the foolish ruler who tried to build a tower without first counting the cost and had to abandon the project halfway through.

Count the cost! If your church feels that this style best fits your vision and goals, then go for it! But do it together as a whole church and be prepared before you launch.

Recruitment Method #7: Volunteer Incentives—This "recruitment" method involves an incentive of some kind. For example, anyone who signs up to work in kids' ministry in the month of March will get a free mug (or cafe gift card, or Bible, etc.). I have seen clever giveaways of gift cards, boxes of candy bars, coffee and donuts, and free breakfast for the whole family every Sunday they volunteer (this one I like, because you help the family get there in the morning)

Pro: You are reminding people that you are there and that you need help. You are showing some creativity and initiative. It serves as a reminder to someone who may have needed that extra nudge to finally get in there and help.

Con: You are bribing people to serve. People need to be taught that serving is just part of being a Christian. But I understand the need to get help in there. We have tried this a few times, and it has not been effective. A person who did not feel any need to serve in kids' ministry before probably won't be swayed by a mug. But it may be worth a try. I would suggest using it, if at all, in collaboration with other methods.

Recruitment Method #8: Volunteers Recruiting Volunteers—Here is an important fact you need to know:

Most of the leaders in your kids' ministry were recruited by someone already in or formerly in your ministry. It's a fact. Most people do not want to serve with strangers. And when they feel overwhelmed in a classroom, their first impulse usually is turn to a friend and say, "Hey, I need help in here. We could do this together." Some of my best teachers over the years have been duos—friends who served together, couples, families, and siblings. Your best recruiters are the ones already *in* your ministry! That is why how you treat your volunteers, stay connected and communicate with them, and publicly show your appreciation is so important. I did a recruitment campaign called Each One Bring One. How it worked was we gave each of our leaders the assignment to recruit one person in a five-week period. We gave the current volunteer the gift card for recruiting a friend. Have you ever noticed that people tend to have friends with similar interests and likes? Do you like your current leaders? Then ask them to replicate themselves. This increases your recruiters from one (you) to your entire volunteer force. Advertise this well, and then keep checking on your leaders to see their progress. The idea is to double your volunteer base in five weeks. This is an idea that I like a lot and plan to use again soon.

Recruitment Method #9: Youth Group and Student Ministries Appeal—"Whoa, wait a minute, Pastor Trisha. I signed up to work with kids. I don't do teenagers." Wrong. Any children's ministry that is cutting edge and growing has learned to effectively plug in and mentor teenagers (see chapter 5 for a great rant on this topic). It is imperative that you develop a great working relationship with the youth pastor and show your face in youth group occasionally to do a "plug" for kids' ministry.

Pros: Students will do all the wild wacky crazy things that your adults may simply refuse to do (for example, dunk tank into ice cubes and Jell-o for missions). They will try new avenues of ministry, like worship, acting, dance, and tech. They are better than you at the tech stuff, but you already knew that. One of my best ProPresenter coordinators was a sixteen-year-old boy. These students have a lot of energy, passion, and creativity. They love to serve and can be amazing anointed workers.

Cons: Sometimes students sign up for anything and everything and then don't show up (adults do this too, however). They can overcommit themselves, stress out, and begin to drop the ball. They have to balance ministry with school, sports, social time, and so on, and they are just starting to learn balance. Many times the young person commits, but if you didn't call a parent and get a commitment from them too, the young person may not be able to get there. Most of them cannot drive, so parent support of their child's ministry commitments is crucial (see sample form in the back for student ministries sign ups). All in all, engaging these dynamic young ministers is worth it. Go after them and let them lead.

Recruitment Method #10: Reaching Outside Your Church—This involves either hiring or finding volunteers outside your church. You can contact Bible colleges in your area and advertise for an intern or volunteer help. To do this you need to call them first and then write up an "ad" that they post. Usually, when you are hiring from outside it is to do a specific job such as Wednesday night nursery, toy cleaning, or worship leading.

Pro: Sometimes you can benefit from a fresh pair of eyes and new talent. Great ideas often come in through an outsider's perspective. Anytime you hire someone, it is a safe bet that person will show up and do their work. I had a lot of peace of mind with the two people hired for Wednesday-night nursery. They were always there; parents loved them, and kids loved the consistency. They were always very professional and thorough. It was a huge relief to not have to recruit for that area. Those two ladies stayed in that role for eighteen years.

Cons: There are lots of cons here, for sure. First, you are lucky to get an intern at all. As I said, there is a huge shortage of kids' ministry interns, and most churches are trying at the Bible colleges and still waiting more than five years a childrens' ministries major. If you get an intern, good for you! The student may not even be a kids' ministry intern, but every little bit helps. Second, you need to find out if the employee's or intern's beliefs line up with those of your church or denomination. They don't go to your church and will be with your kids. (Yes, give them a background check too). I remember our senior pastor hiring a temporary youth pastor from an interdenominational youth ministry agency in our county. Months later we found out he was teaching a doctrine totally opposite of what our church believes. Parents were not happy and neither was the pastor. Find out what they believe! Thirdly, once you start paying people, others may expect pay as well. You will eventually have to draw a line. Fourth, interns and outside volunteers are a Band-Aid; they are there for a time and then gone. They are not a long-term solution. If this is a desperation move, you still have to find permanent leaders for those areas. But that temporary person may buy you time to create excitement and kick-start that area!

Recruitment Technique #11: Big-Event Launching Pad—This is when you use your biggest kids outreach, such as VBS or the Christmas musical, as a medium to invite in new volunteers.

Pros: All of my largest recruitments, the ones that brought in not only a lot of new leaders but that brought in our high-capacity leaders for the long haul, came right off a successful big kids' event. Why? Remember when I said all great recruitment flows from vision that makes people want to be a part of a winning team? Imagine that you've have just had your best kids' Christmas musical ever. You have a packed house and people are touched on an emotional level by the amazing ministry they have just experienced, done by and for kids. Then you, or your lead pastor, get up front and mention, "Hey, if you would like more information on being a part of a stellar program like this, please sign up at the booth before leaving today." No apologizing or begging. Your kids involved in ministry have said volumes more than all the programs and video appeals ever could. This is just being strategic and thinking ahead. Most successful kids' programs have two to three outreaches every year. Get the most for your time and make sure you give people a chance to sign on then too.

Cons: Sometimes people will sign up in the heat of the moment and then later go home and realize they are overcommitted. This can happen in any appeal. Other times, they sign on to be a part of a musical or artistic outreach and find out you only have three a year. They may not want to be a week-to-week teacher. My suggestion is to have a variety of positions available for which people can sign up, both one-time opportunities and long-term positions. For example, I have drama and dance teams throughout the year and opportunities to serve in our city. Give potential leaders a variety of ways to use their giftings.

Recruitment Technique #12: A Concentrated All-Church Push— Examples of this technique include a volunteer month, a parent-serve month, or a kids' ministry-serve month. Quite simply, this method involves combining several methods just mentioned above in one all-church effort from every angle to recruit  volunteers for kids' ministry. This means being strategic, and planning months ahead. This means scheduling all of your onboarding processes and orientations in a streamlined manner to directly coincide with all this recruiting! For example, if the recruitment is every weekend in the month of March, your orientation should be around April 2 (not too close or too far from the end of your campaign), with your best current volunteers there in force for orientation and trainings. You need to have your plan ready to have all those people in place before the end of April. You also need to coordinate with all other areas of the church that are willing to partner with you. Remember, when one of us wins, we all win. To have an amazing recruitment, you are going to have to work with whoever is over facilities (what tables, rooms, booths, equipment are you going to need? Get those requests in!). You will probably need help from the student ministries department, perhaps to help man booths, advertise, or perform on stage. You will need to connect with the church's service planning teams to coordinate with them on service videos, media, and kids' performing. There is a lot to do!

First look at your church calendar and decide your target date to have all of the new volunteers in place, working in your ministry. (Yes, I know you want to say tomorrow, but we're not talking strategies for next week; we are talking recruiting for the long term. It is a mistake to recruit people and have no plan to use them in ministry.) So how do you pick a realistic target date? I look ahead to the next very busy time when I already know we'll need a lot of help. For us there are two: September and the fall kids' ministry kickoffs, and the whole month surrounding Easter. We already know that we need those volunteers in place, trained, and ready to go by then. What is the busiest time of the year at your church for the children's ministry? This is important to know. Then, starting with that target date, back it up and create a timeline. Summer is tricky, because many people are on vacation and do not like coming in for special meetings. But here is a sample of what I have done recruiting volunteers for our fall season:

July 5–6: Media piece/video for main service (best kids' services, volunteer testimonies), signup in bulletin, to be placed in the offering. All ushers wear blue for "Pray for PowerHouse Kids' Weekend."

July 12–13: Kids perform a worship song/dance for main service; sign up in bulletin, to be placed in the offering. Hand out prayer bookmark for the kids' ministries. Begin calling everyone who signed up to help and giving them information on getting involved and orientation. Start calling every parent/guardian in the church asking them to serve in kids' ministry. (I use an "ask" and an "expectation," for parents to serve in children's ministry, but I don't go as far as an enforced co-op.)

July 19–20: Ministry Fair—Kids' ministry booth features live puppeteers, full body costume characters, a photo booth, video of best services, and fresh-baked cookies. Everyone who signs up receives a coupon for the church's coffee cafe. Call everyone who has signed up. Follow up. Get teams of people following up.

July 26–27: I speak for offering in the main sanctuary, making a pulpit appeal for leaders. We also announce Each One Bring One challenge for our volunteers. Finish all calls and follow up that week.

August 3: Orientation for all new volunteers. Fingerprinting and background checks take place at orientation. (No one serves until a background check comes back clean.)

August 6: Makeup orientation.

August 10: Training and shadowing.

August 13: Makeup training and shadowing, call all applicant references.

August 17: More training and shadowing.

August 20: More training and shadowing, evaluate who is serving where. Move new volunteers to better positions if needed.

August 24: All-volunteer rally and appreciation.

August 31: Massive back-to-school musical and kickoff; another volunteer appeal.

Sept. 6: Late orientation, training, fingerprinting.

This timeline works well for January too. Sometimes it works better in October or March because there are not as many people gone. However with a January launch, you do have to factor in that most of December will be gone with holidays and school functions. So pick your timeline well.

Pros: This kind of strategic, well-planned, well-executed recruitment makes a lasting impact on your entire congregation, not just those who sign up. It works. And when done well, it wins credibility for you and the ministry you are working hard to grow. So plan, collaborate, set a timeline, make it excellent, and get those volunteer, partner leaders you so badly need. I love this method because it concentrates your efforts for maximum impact and momentum. Remember how they say people need to hear something seven times to remember and act on it? This gets your message out to the most people in the best ways possible.

Cons: It's a lot of work. We all want to sit there on a Saturday night wishing on that first star and suddenly see help appear out of nowhere. But it doesn't work that way. Creating a team of quality children's leaders can happen, but like everything worth fighting for in this life, it is a lot of work. How badly do you want that help in your kids' areas? Is it worth putting in all that time, and all that work? I say, absolutely.

171

Last but not least, let's address an elephant in the room: children's ministry versus child care. There is this battle raging in churches across the United States right now, and it's directly related to the recruiting we just discussed. Sometime in the late 1980s, when the church-consumer mentality hit its peak, the church began offering free child care for every event during the week. As time has gone by, parents have come to expect free child care for church events. And this problem is further complicated by churches having more and more events, sometimes every night of the week. Many times when a new event or study is announced, child care is just expected, and the new unsuspecting kids' ministry leader has no idea that he or she was supposed to find babysitters for every event. I think at this point, you realize how passionate I am about children's and family ministry. I believe in making a clear separation between ministry and babysitting. We do not take kids in another room and "entertain" them or "keep them quiet" while the church does important ministry. We are reaching kids for Christ, and every moment counts. When I first came on staff at my third pastorate, I had no idea my team and I would be expected to find babysitters for Bible studies and events many nights of the week. It was beyond overwhelming. We were already using all of the above strategies just to try to cover our four weekend services and our midweek service. Our focus had to be recruiting, training, working with our leaders and parents for our weekend programs, not being on the

(teaching   puppetry   at   a   teen   challenge   center   in   Africa)

phone all day begging for sitters for all of the nightly events. Everything finally came to a head when I came to a leader's meeting one Tuesday morning and laid yet another event on the table. One of my amazing hard-working leaders put her head on the table and started crying. The next day she turned in her resignation. There was no doubt in my mind that she left due to feeling overwhelmed, at least in part, by the child care duties. We were still not able to turn things around in a week, but her departure gave me incentive to keep trying. We were able to completely separate children's ministry from babysitting, though it took a year and half of hard work to do so. And it was worth

EVERY meeting and presentation to make that happen. Most growing churches are now having to address this issue. If you haven't read it already, I highly recommend the book *Simple Church: Returning to God's Process for Making Disciples*, by Thom S. Rainer and Eric Geiger (2011, B&H Publishing). Here is the reality: our churches need to do fewer events with more quality, and we need to start streamlining the events we are already doing. We moved almost all Bible studies and events to times we were already doing children's ministry. We then started letting people know that we would no longer be providing child care for events or classes that did not include the whole church. People were surprised at first, but we patiently worked with them and eventually they caught on. I recruited an amazing young woman who took over as "Events Child Care Coordinator." Her volunteer position is to find babysitters for all-church events only which is an average of two events per month. She also focuses on recruiting and using babysitters who are not from our pool of every-week children's ministry teachers! Some examples of all church events are: What We Believe 101, the Annual Church Business Meeting, and the Live Worship Album Recording Night. We created and implemented preplanning forms that helped her to plan ahead and stay fully staffed. It also kept other departments of the church from asking for "10 babysitters this Friday night."

The effect of taking babysitting off our hands for our staff and our ministries was beyond description. Instead of finding babysitters every night of the week, we now rarely need to do so. We focus all our energy on children's ministry, filling classes with amazing leaders, training those leaders, and connecting with parents. As a result, my staff, my team, and I are less stressed, and all of our areas have grown quickly under this laser-focused attention.

Why should your church consider limiting its babysitting services?

A. We were spreading ourselves and our volunteers too thin. At our church, we were having to ask our same pool of overworked, overcommitted volunteers to bail us out and babysit weeknight after weeknight. We lost two great weekend kids' ministry leaders because they were burned out babysitting during the week. Do not let this happen. Your weekend kids' ministry is far too important to sacrifice for any group's babysitting. Having trouble recruiting? It's time to cut out recruiting for nonpriorities. No matter how hard you try, you cannot do everything. And if you try to do it all, you will stumble through it poorly with fried, unhappy leaders. Choose the few things you are going to do, and do them well. Your priority needs to be your weekend and midweek services.

B. All that babysitting can be a liability for the church. Some churches are getting sued because of things happening during these largely unstructured babysitting times on church property. Do we really want to be liable for what happens with kids in church classrooms after office hours? This is usually when items go missing, are broken or destroyed, or a child gets hurt on the church property with no staff member present. Not good.

C. This is a great opportunity to let people see the value of the children's ministry at your church. Your first step here needs to be to vision cast, lead UP, to your senior leader and leadership team. This can take time, patience, and effort. Then, as a church team, start streamlining what you do, and being more effective at the few things you continue to do. Be prepared for a lot of arguments and excuses such as:

"But we have to have child care or they won't show up." This is true in some cases. There are families that will not attend if no babysitting is provided. So start putting all of these meetings and events when children's ministry is already in session, such as Sundays or midweek. It is better to streamline events for families anyway. For your events and meetings, you will have to specify and advertise whether

you will be providing child care. If families know ahead of time, it gives them time to plan.

"It is what we have always done. Now people expect free babysitting at every event. There are no other options." The truth is people can learn to do things a different way. It takes time, love, and patience. What did the average family do before we offered child care at every event? What do parents do now when they have a meeting for work, an outing, a PTA gathering, or a date night? They get a babysitter. All of these other events do not provide free babysitting; only the church does. The time has come to rethink that policy. *"Well it involves kids, so it's the kids' leader's job."* That is as ridiculous as saying, "Well, I need a teacher for fourth grade. I need an adult so that's your job." This is why job descriptions matter. We are a team, and we need to work together. You cannot perpetuate the outdated thinking that you and your team babysit while the "real staff" does ministry. What your team does each week is far beyond babysitting. Do ministry, and do it together as a church team. Note that over time, people came to expect free babysitting at every church event. Over time, then, you can change that expectation. Helping your people to become active participants in their kids' ministry is a process, but it's worth it.

So is your head spinning yet? I hope you have some good ideas to get you started. My bottom line is this: You *can* do strategic, well-planned, well-executed volunteer recruitment. It can be successful and make a lasting impact on your entire congregation, not just those who sign up. You can win credibility for you and the ministry you are working so hard to grow. Feel free to use and adapt the methods you feel may work for you, and try some that are not listed here. Keep praying and believing that God wants to minister to these kids even more than we do, and that He is calling people right now to be a part of this ministry. Plan, collaborate, set a timeline, and make it excellent. Go get those volunteers and leaders you need so badly. Now we'll look at what to do with those teams once you've got them.

Chapter 7 Turn Signals

Communication Skills That Work

Kerri checked her teeth one more time in the mirror. "Okay, no lipstick on my teeth." Placing her clammy palms on the cool sink counter she faced her reflection in the mirror. "You can do this, Kerri," she began her pep talk. "This is going to be a very big day. You are going to do just fine."

Kerri had many talents—organizing, fundraising, and she made a to-die-for cinnamon apple strudel. But two things in this world terrified Kerri and haunted her dreams: (1) that a house fire would destroy her vast shoe collection, and (2) public speaking. At this very moment in the women's bathroom near the elementary classrooms, she would almost rather face the shoe-devouring fire over speaking at this parent-volunteer orientation. Almost. This was certainly something to be excited about. After several months of work and research, they had mission and vision statements for the kids' ministry and were about to launch a new curriculum. Kerri realized that the church needed parents and volunteers onboard 100 percent if the curriculum switch was really going to work. They would have to partner together to recruit all the new leaders they were going to need. All this excitement after today would certainly lead to new people and growth—a first in a long time for this kids' area. She really hoped they would have time to get to all the questions before their forty-five-minute meeting was up. Taking one more deep breath, she checked her teeth one more time, grabbed her well-organized notes (sorted and copied for everyone—did she bring enough?) and hurried down the hall to room 507. This was it. To her surprise she realized as she turned the door knob and pushed open the door that she was excited that she finally had good news for this crowd today; good news worth calling this meeting and facing a packed room (gulp). Time to push open this door to new frontiers.

This excitement was immediately extinguished when she entered the room and saw only two people there. Was she in the wrong room? No, one of the two people was Karen, who had helped her so much in selecting a curriculum. Karen, a retired school teacher, had come in just to support Kerri on a big day. The other woman was new to the church and had three small children. Where was everyone? Didn't they hear the pulpit announcement? Just this week, Kerri had received (or overheard) three parent complaints that no one knew what was going on or what the new curriculum was going to be. Wouldn't those people want to be here? The parents, volunteers, and staff need to know this information. But how can I get it to them and get their feedback if they don't come to the meeting? This is a disaster!

Is any of this sounding familiar? Most children's leaders have lived this scenario: parents and volunteers complaining that "they have no idea what is going on"; "I didn't get the training I needed"; "I had no clue we were even doing a VBS"; "I wish we had been told that the service times would be changing." And then almost no one shows up to the informational meetings!

I recently asked a group of lead pastors what they are most looking for in a children's pastor (they were all launching a new search for a children's pastor). To my surprise, one of the top qualities each listed was "the ability to communicate well with parents and volunteers." A friend of mine had three children's ministry interviews in one week. Each pastor asked, "What is your plan to communicate with parents and volunteers?"

With "family ministry" being so central to more and more churches, it is imperative that you communicate well and often with parents to truly be partners with them in their child's spiritual formation. The more volunteers you recruit, the more teams and shifts you create, the more adept you must become at communicating clearly and effectively with your volunteer base. Gone are the days when a children's leader could get away with saying, "I only speak to kids, not adults." You must be an effective communicator to adults for the kids' department to thrive and grow.

Some information—the very important turns and changes in the ministry, whether they be leadership changes, curriculum or scheduling changes—must be clearly communicated to the parents and leaders. The timely relaying of information is essential partnering. But how do you go about relaying it to parents and volunteers? Remember what I told you about people needing to see, hear, or experience something seven times before it sinks in? Remember when we talked about the barrage of information that we are buried under every day? You are going to have to be strategic, persistent, and consistent to get information across. So I encourage you to use some or all of these methods to convey information:

1. *Live meetings.* This is typically the old-school method of "letting the parents and volunteers know" what is coming up. This is the one Kerri was using. It is not a method to use weekly and should only be used to convey something of great importance (examples: major curriculum change, service times change, key leader stepping down, brand new security procedures that affect everyone). Here are some tips to make sure your live meeting is a success:

A. Advertise it at least one month in advance, and advertise it in many ways.

B. Be specific. Who is supposed to be present? When you say "parent meeting," is that *all* parents? Parents of kids up to twelve years old? Parents of preschoolers? Parents of fourth and fifth graders? Parents are understandably irritated if they clear their schedule (especially if they paid a sitter) to go to your important meeting, only to find out you didn't mean them. Be specificabout the location. Can parents find that room if they are new? What time is it? Is there child care provided? How long will the meeting be? Why should I be there? Indicate why the meeting is important, like a leadership or curriculum change, but don't go into too much detail. One church I visited handed out a leaflet during the service that said, "Parent meeting right after service in the Garden room." Parents were in a mass of confusion. I heard them saying, "Meeting right after which service?" "Why do we have to go? Is the pastor leaving?" "I'm a parent of two junior-highers. Do I have to go?" "I'm new. Where on earth is the Garden room?" That parent meeting was a total disaster. I heard that the youth pastor who called the meeting never made that mistake again. But sadly the congregation didn't forget it soon either.

B. Be respectful of people's time. I didn't fully understand this when I was a new children's pastor, but now that I have kids of my own, it makes more sense. For example, do everything in your power not to take another night of the week. Parents and volunteers are already, on average, gone at least five nights a week with church, sports, recitals, plays, and so on. If you pick a night during the week, unless it is an emergency meeting, many will not be there. And the ones who show up want a sense that this was important to take some of the only family time they might have that whole week. Try to have the meeting when they are at church already—first service, if you have two (this takes care of someone to watch their kids too); directly after a service (some will complain about lunch); before or after midweek service (some will complain if it gets late for their kids to be out on a school night). No matter when you pick, someone will complain, so you cannot please everyone, but try to be considerate. They will already be resentful of you if they feel you do not care about their family time, and you need them on your team!

C. I also do not recommend sending out a survey asking what time to have the meeting. You will get thirty-seven different answers; one person will get their way (and probably not show up) and the rest will think, "no one cares that I filled out the survey" and not show up. I personally ask one or two people I trust and then make a decision and stick with it.

D. This is going to sound awful, like bribery, because it is bribery, but we always have more people show up when we offer food. So we offer refreshments if we really need people to hear what we have to say. Advertise that you will have refreshments!

E. Honor their time by keeping to the point and being brief. Stick to your notes. Better to end early than irritate people with a never-ending meeting. Yes, you probably have a lot of things on your heart to go

185

over, that need changing in the kids' area, but this is not the time for that. Stick to the reason you have them there. If you don't, they won't come to the next one.

F. Do not give out information early. This is an important lesson I learned as a children's pastor. When I went on staff at a certain church, I was told that "no one shows up for parent or volunteer meetings." I wondered why. Then I called a meeting about an important security change. Right away the phone calls started coming in. "Um, I can't make the meeting. What's the announcement?" "We are out of town. Just give me the details." Right away I realized why no one came to the meetings. There was no reason to. They got a few abbreviated details over the phone, passed them on to each other, and skipped the meetings. The meetings were no longer of any importance. People were shocked as I told them one by one, "I'm sorry to hear that. This will be a very important change happening. I want it to first be presented to the people present. Wouldn't want it to get out over the grapevine. I highly suggest you get with one of those who were there after you return and get their notes. That's a bummer, because I really would have liked your input. But maybe after you get back you can make an appointment with me and I can try to catch you up." This had a dramatic effect. First they pushed for more info. I held to my guns very politely and wished them a great trip. Word got out that something "big" was going on. Nine times out of ten "their schedule just cleared up." And I spoke to a packed house. Give them a reason to show up and be really present. Ask yourself these questions: Is this change something you want discussed in the court of public opinion before you even present it? Do you want to give ammo to those who resist change? Do you want parents and volunteers serving with only partial or possibly incorrect information? Do not call a parent or volunteer meeting for any petty reason. But when you determine that the change affects everyone and they need to be there, do not give out an abbreviated version before the event.

G. Give people a chance to provide input, feedback, and ask questions. Be prepared to give well-researched answers to their questions. If you do not know the answer, take down the questioner's name and respond, "I'm not sure, but I will find out." You will gain parent support and more volunteers if you allow honest feedback and questions. I usually take notes during that time.

H. Do not let anyone monopolize the discussion. Especially if you are a young or new children's leader, stay in charge of that meeting and keep it on the task at hand. Do not allow the topic to get derailed to something else. Do not let it be a forum for debate. Your response when challenged sets the tone for your ministry. Also, don't be defensive or argumentative. You're not *trying* to lead the meeting, you *are* leading it. It is not the place to aim anything at anyone or have a great big public argument. There are people in this world who jump at the chance for public drama. That is the biggest drawback to having a parent or volunteer meeting. Don't give anyone a pulpit for a public drama. Shut down anything nasty as soon as it starts. You can say something like this:

"That is a whole different discussion, for another time. Make an appointment to see me about that" (they usually won't because they want an audience).

"Wow that sounds intense. Why don't you see me about that when we are done."

"Okay, let's hear what some other parents think about this topic."

"Interesting, but for the sake of time, let's stay on topic."

"I hear you. I'd love to talk with you more about that. Here is why the church made the decision that it made. Here is the plan."

"I know you probably have more you would like to share on this topic. Good thing I am putting my email up on the screen, and I would like to hear from you and several of these others. I am also handing out these feedback forms. Please put your name on it if you wish to be contacted. Everyone please fill out a feedback form and leave it on your chair." (Instead of public meetings, some churches now use only email and forms for feedback. I understand why.)

Remember that the purpose of the meeting is to communicate vision, convey information, and occasionally to garner feedback. It is not a debate. Do not imply that the church's decisions are being debated or being voted on. You are letting them know that a decision has been made or that a change is coming. Never use one of these meetings to attack someone or any area of the church. Do not retaliate in any way if someone makes a snide comment. You set the tone. Make sure the parent or volunteer meeting is a positive, uplifting, and beneficial experience for everyone involved. Make all of your parents and volunteers eager to be at any meeting you call.

2. *Pulpit announcements.* This involves announcing your change to the children's area, policy, or an upcoming meeting from the pulpit during services. Too many children's leaders fall into the trap of thinking that one pulpit announcement will carry all the needed information to everyone who needs it. True, the pulpit announcement (or pre- or midservice media) has the potential to reach the most people in the

congregation all at once. However, the average American church-goer only attends once or twice a month. (See statistics cited in the vision chapter.) So, if you are really lucky, your announcement about that volunteer "classroom discipline class" only got to about half your volunteers. Since some of them were in the bathroom, or serving in a class, or running late that morning, you didn't come close to getting it across to all of them. If you make the mistake of only using the pulpit announcement, you will get several "But nobody told me!" responses. The pulpit announcement is a great tool in conjunction with other methods. But it is usually difficult to get across all the detail information from the pulpit. Imagine hearing this from the stage:

> Integrating Children with Special Needs into our Classrooms is a special training we are having for new and returning volunteers who lead in our second- to fifth-grade classes. The class will be meeting for the next three Saturdays from 10:00–11:30 a.m., lunch provided, and the cost is six dollars. It meets in room 409 for the first two Saturdays, and room 510 on the third Saturday.

Did you just memorize all that? No way. The rest of the church didn't either. So how about this instead:

Attention elementary volunteers, serving in second to fifth grades! We need *you* at an important training coming up Saturdays in September, all about ministering to our special needs kids. For more information, go to www.awesomechurch.org/kids. (Yeah, I just made that up.)

Bottom line: the main weekend service is a great place to get people's attention; it is *not* the place to unload all the details. So you have to tell them *where* to get all those details. I highly recommend a website or Facebook page. I always cringe when a children's leader says from the stage, "Please come see me for more information." See you where? Do all of these people have your phone number? If so, why do they all have your phone number? Do you ever make it through a dinner with your family uninterrupted? If you are married, do you plan to stay married? (I'm looking for a yes answer here.) Can you keep that up when your ministry grows? (This one is a no.) Some churches put up a booth with all information in the foyer. Not a bad idea. The drawback is that when they get home and do not remember what you said, they still have to call you anyway.

3. *Websites are always open. Facebook is free.* Remember when I said to update it often? You should be updating your ministry website or Facebook or Twitter at least monthly. I update mine every week (or twice a week). It is a good idea to "overcommunicate" your changes with parents and volunteers! When I first opened the Facebook page for our kids' ministry, I didn't expect a whole lot. I just wanted to put up cool pictures, but I was surprised at the result. As word spread that I was updating weekly, many parents told me they got all of their information on what was going on in the kids' ministry from that Facebook page. Then volunteers began checking it every week too. I posted our Wednesday-night theme nights, our parent meetings, our volunteer needs, our auditions for the Christmas play and more. I got in the habit of posting every week, and they all got in the habit of reading it every week. The most amazing thing happened: we were communicating and connecting. The number of phone calls I received

every day with questions was cut by almost 75 percent. Parents and volunteers preferred looking at Facebook on their phone at work. New parents will ask, "When is that fourth- and fifth-grade team meeting?" And all the other parents say, "Oh, you need to get on Facebook." And the new parent pulls out his or her phone and subscribes right then. The new family is connected to what is going on and to a community of staff and other families. As you grow, you must find newer, better ways to deliver concise information to more people. I still change it up to make things fresh. For example, sometimes I announce things in a status, or show a picture of our intern getting dunked to remind parents of the special offering tonight, or a video of my Wednesday-night leader talking about training. Currently we are using video updates only occasionally, but I am considering the possibility of a weekly video update. Occasionally we even post silly, special songs. Be creative!

Above all, you need to intentionally create a hub for information, a creative place to efficiently disseminate information 24/7, and even provide the opportunity to print forms and documents. The more ways you communicate effectively, the better. Avoid the trap of saying, "Well we know everybody here, so we just tell a couple people and it's all good. They all know already." It is that kind of thinking that will make guests feel awkward and completely out of place. They will not know what is going on and will not have an outlet to find needed information. They won't be back. If you want your church to grow, you have to start planning and acting on your plan for growth. For example, if you are a church of two hundred and keep communicating and planning for 200 people, you will remain a church of 200 (best-case scenario). To grow to a church of 350, you have to start now, acting, planning and communicating as if you are already there. Stop for just a second here: it's epiphany time. How many does your church run now, on average? _____ When your kids' ministry begins growing, and working along with an active church, your church can grow quickly. If your church grew by just 10 percent in the next six months, adding new people, who do not know the culture of your church, what would your average be? _____ How are you getting ready for that leap now? What needs to change in the way you communicate to parents and volunteers to be the church of that second number? _____

That is your challenge. Start setting great communications practices now, to be ready for solid partnering then.

4. *Robo calling.* There are a few of these calling systems. For example, Call 'em All, which we use at our church. You record a phone message and a service auto dials every phone number in your church's system

and leaves your message. This is an attempt to communicate with people in your church who do not routinely look at email or Facebook. The positive is that you can "call" a nearly infinite number of people all at once. We use it in conjunction with other methods, primarily as a reminder, of things like a special leadership meeting, camp registration due, the kickoff of VBS, and so on. I am not, however, a huge fan of robo calling, due to its drawbacks. For one thing, what do most people do when they receive a robo call? I hang up. I find them irritating. A lot of our parents admit, they hang up on the robo calls. But even the first few seconds of the message sometimes serves as a reminder: "Oh yeah, I need to get that registration in today." Secondly, most of these services are not free. You pay for them per minute. Facebook and email are free. Thirdly, because it costs money and people generally hate these calls, you have to keep your message very short and clear. Make sure your message is understandable and concise. For example:

> Hi, this is Pastor Trish, just reminding you that this Wednesday night, which is tomorrow night, is the deadline to turn in your camp forms, with the twenty-dollar registration hold fee. Turn in your forms and fees in the strongbox by door 6. To download and print forms, or pay online, or get more

information, go to _____ today. Thanks, and
God bless your day.

Direct them to a permanent information hub such as a website or
Facebook, because they probably will not remember everything you
say in the message. This is usually not the place (and you do not have
the time) to relay all of the nitty gritty details, but it serves as a
reminder. Fourth, a robo call usually sparks questions. Before you send
out the calls, make sure you have answers to frequently asked questions
on your website, Facebook page, and especially to whoever is
answering the phones at your church. We always get a flood of calls at
the front office: "Oh, hey, I just got this robo call at work. Can I just
send the registration form and check with my kid tomorrow night? Can
I write a check? Who do I make it out to?" This puts the receptionist or
whoever is answering the phone in an awkward spot if you are in a
meeting or home for the day. I print out FAQs for the front desk before
we send out the calls, and I also post them on our website and
Facebook. Fifth, the database you use needs constant maintenance. One
problem we run into is that parents do not want to give us their phone
number. Sometimes the family moves, changes cell companies, and just
forgets to give the church their new number. Is someone making sure
all those new families and visitors are in the database? And there will

always be some entries that are incorrect. Even with constant maintenance, you cannot rely on robo calling to reach every family. There will always be some who say, "You never called me." That is why I try to use several methods to (I hope) reach as many as humanly possible.

If you truly want to partner with parents and volunteers, you have to become an expert at connecting with them. Unanswered questions just lead to distrust and frustration and ultimately disconnection.

5. *Personal phone calls.* This is when you personally call each person to tell them something important. Use this method with discretion. This is not for letting 100 people know about a meeting. Yikes! Also, never do a confrontation this way. Confrontations should always be in private and in person, not over email, phone, or through another person. But let's say you want a meeting with your six key Wednesday-night leaders to plan next year. There are only a few people who need to know, and it's important that they are all there. This isn't something to do over an email. A personal ask or a personal phone call is best. Need to cancel that important meeting with your key leaders? Don't trust that to email either. Nothing is worse than changing your whole schedule, getting a sitter for your kids, making the drive to

church, and you are the only one there. And then hearing, "Well I emailed you." Pick up the phone and call. If church is being canceled due to weather, call your key leaders as soon as you know, and ask them to call their leaders. If someone calls you, call them back (sounds obvious, but I've been surprised). A good rule of thumb is to return the phone call within twenty-four hours. This is just good communication—a necessary skill to connect with and keep parents and volunteers. It is surprising to me how often new kids' leaders do not realize that there is still so much power in simply picking up the phone and making that call. It is more effective and personal than email. One time both of our special needs class teachers called in sick on Sunday morning. We were not able to fill the class on such short notice. My elementary leader called the three families that usually come to the class. It took just a few minutes. One mom was so touched. She said, "Thank you for taking the time to call us. Our son is so disabled that it takes us thirty minutes just to get him ready, and get him in the vehicle. And we live 45 minutes away. Without the special needs teacher he is used to, church would have been miserable for us, and we would have had to turn right around and go back home. Thank you for letting us know. It makes us feel like you guys really care about us, and that we are a part of this church now." That's the power of picking up the phone.

6. *The handout.* You may be surprised to hear that I used to not like the handout. We all get bombarded with paper from the schools, church, and sports. My two kids average fourteen pieces of paper each day just from school. I admit I don't read them all. I get overwhelmed and just skim and I throw most of it away before I drown in a sea of papers. So you would think a handout at church would not be very effective. But when a friend of mine told me to put my important parent announcement on a small quarter sheet handout and put it in the parents' hands at checkout, I was skeptical. I dragged my feet, because it sounded like extra work for nothing. But I was wrong. (I tell my friends that I have to be wrong about once a year so I don't get raptured early; that's a joke!) As long as we keep it short, stick to the details, use it as a reminder, and point readers to the website, it seems to be working! Parents read through it, stick the flyer on the fridge, and look for these flyers whenever a new one comes out. Here are a few examples:

Attention parents: REMINDER—Next week on Wednesday night (March 13) every child needs to bring a box of macaroni and cheese for our food pantry drive. Want more information? Go to _____ Thanks!

199

For Christmas play dress rehearsal this Tuesday night 7:00 p.m., your child needs a white shirt, black pants, tennis shoes, hair pulled back in a ponytail, and a snack to pass. Want more information on the play, the rehearsals, and more? Go to _____Thanks!

Reminder, parent meeting next Sunday second service (10:00 am) in 506 for all parents of preschoolers, regarding the hire of our new preschool leader.

If you only do this for one weekend, you will hit less than half of your families and leaders, so it works best as a reminder, not a stand-alone announcement. Don't use handouts to relay important messages for the first time, like Pastor James is stepping down, but we hired Pastor Judy last week." This will just create confusion, distrust, and leave unanswered questions. Here is a better handout: "Reminder—there is an important preschool parent meeting next Sunday at 10:00 a.m. in 506, regarding an upcoming leadership change."

My verdict is that handouts can be useful tools if you keep them short and use them as reminders.

7. Snail mail and the letter home. I reserve letters home to each family for very special occasions, such as introducing a new staff member, launching a new curriculum, or an invitation to a volunteer banquet. The letter home carries more weight than an email and provides a hard copy for parents to refer to later. Snail mail is not a great way to communicate "tight turns," meaning something coming up this weekend. A lot of families (again because of the deluge of paper) throw out anything that looks like an ad or another credit card offer. Some families only go through their mail on weekends. Another problem you run into is the database issue and not having correct addresses for everyone, especially as people grow wary of giving out personal information. You also won't have addresses for some of your visitors. The result is you won't be able to reach all of your audience with only a letter home. Mailing letters is going to cost you money too. So it can get cost-prohibitive if you try this every week. But the snail mail letter is the place to distribute detailed vision, written policies, schedules, and the like.

8. Newsletters. Newsletters are typically sent monthly or quarterly to parents and volunteers. The one I use is from Group Publishing, and I highly recommend their Parenting Christian Kids monthly newsletter. I love that it comes over email set up in full color and visually sharp.

You take out the sections you do not want and add what you want the parents of your church to know. Then you can send it out over email, snail mail, post it to your website or Facebook page, or hand it out. I like Group's because it comes with articles on current movies and TV shows, comics, articles on parenting and child development, a blank church calendar that we fill in, and other features. We added a back page with an article from one of our staff and a "spotlight corner" about one of our volunteers! You can purchase twelve months of these from Group or another publisher. You can also try making your own if you are feeling ambitious. I love this tool for connecting with parents and leaders. The only drawback is that you do not get a direct line of interaction and feedback. You can't see who is looking at it, foster discussion, or hear what they think about it—unless you post it on Facebook (great idea).

9. *The email blast.* We are finally to my personal favorite form of communication with parents and volunteers. Surprised? Here's why I love the email blast: I can contact the majority of parents and volunteers in seconds, I have a written record of what I sent, and it's free. Here's how it works. The hardest part is the set up and maintenance of the database. (We use Fellowship One). First, you set up a group in your database of all the email addresses of every family

in your ministry. I've even done this with Google for free for churches that don't have a database. Yes, it's a pain in the neck, but it's worth it. You have to keep it updated with new families and changed emails. Then you have to let your families and volunteers know when you will be sending out this email blast. I have several different groups that I send out each week, for example, fine arts, worship team, weekend teachers, midweek teachers, parent forum, and outreach events. I send out my email blasts every Tuesday by 5:00 p.m. rain or shine. When I am sick or on vacation, I either write it ahead of time and set it to go out or I have someone send it for me. The key here is consistency. Why? I am about to give you another key for great parent and volunteer communication. Key number 1 was "Build a hub for communicating." Key number 2 is "Create a consistent flow of communication." You have to choose which method of communication you will use most for relaying information and then use it consistently. I know that I already told you that you will need to become a ninja at ALL of these modes of connecting, and that is the truth. People communicate in many different ways and are barraged with so much information these days, you must become adept in using all methods, especially for big changes and events. But for your weekly volunteer and parent communications you need one method that is your consistent go-to. No matter which method you pick, someone will complain, "I don't read handouts," or, "We are not at church every Sunday," or, "I forget to pick up the newsletter," or, "I never listen to my voicemail," and so on. No method is going to be everyone's favorite. But you need to choose one anyway and stick with it. Due to the sheer number of people we need to communicate with every week—276 volunteers and the parents of 600 kids—I chose the email blast because I can reach a large number of people at one time, and they have a written record to keep and refer to. At first, when I started sending these out every Tuesday several years ago, I had people complain "Oh, I never check email," or, "I don't want to get email," or, "Just call me or mail it to me." Keep in mind that there is a marked difference between the communication for a major change or a special event; for those, you do need to use every form of communication. But for your regular weekly, biweekly, or monthly communication, you need to streamline. Be careful of the precedent you set. If you give in and call two people and send it over mail to three people, and email fourteen people, you will run yourself ragged trying to keep track of who wants which kind of communication. As you grow, this becomes impossible, not to mention how all this running and people-pleasing can waste so much of your time and resources. Bottom line: Pick your form of usual communication and stick to it. Even now, I answer the people who sign on and say, "Oh, I don't check email, just call me," like this:

"Oh, so sorry about that. We send out our communication with all the important details and updates every Tuesday at 5:00 p.m. over email because it works for the rest of our team. It would be far too much detail for a phone call. I would highly suggest you get with someone who has email each week to get all the information, or you may get really behind on all that is happening." At first they look surprised, but every single time they get an email or learned to read the ones from me. If you are planning to grow, and I hope you are, then you cannot cater to each person's preferred method for your week-to-week communications. The email blast has been working for us because we strive to be rigidly consistent. Over time, parents and volunteers began to count on that email every week for the details, vision casting, inspiration, thank you's, testimonies, and so on. People are eager to read it and get on the list if they are new. The result of holding my ground, being thorough and consistent, and faithful to communicate is that I can speak to almost one thousand people in about fifteen minutes with one email. Everyone then has all the details in writing to print and post on the fridge. They can reply to the email with questions, comments, or suggestions, inviting feedback and two-way communication. This is a huge win for you, the volunteers, parents, and your church as a whole. The drawbacks are keeping the database updated all the time, and the people who say, "I'm not getting the emails" (99 percent of the time it is in their junk mail and they need to change their settings to allow it, or the email address in the system is incorrect). But email blasts are my favorite go-to for regular communications.

10. Texting- This is a newer one and can be used much like the email blast. The major difficulties are people not wanting to give out their phone number, and people not updating their number when it changes. But some churches LOVE this option.

No matter which method you use to communicate, have a proofreader or two whom you trust go over the text before you send it out. Try to think of all the questions that might possibly come up. What would a new family get from reading your handout? How can they get questions answered? Are you giving out too little detail? Too much? A critical look at everything cuts down on the confusion, frustration, and floods of questions coming your way. More importantly, well-done communication builds your credibility and trust, and you'll build your team.

What makes every day at your job, your church, or your ministry worthwhile and pleasant isn't the color of the carpet or the room where you minister. What makes doing ministry a wonderful experience are those with whom you minister. I don't remember all the programs I have done through the years, or paperwork I have filled out, or the meetings I have attended. But I *do* remember those "God moments" ministering to a child who just lost a grandparent. I remember parent advisory board brainstorming sessions ending with meaningful prayer times. I remember exchanging creative ideas (and a lot of laughter) with my staff or department heads. I have never regretted one moment that I spent pouring into someone's life or letting them speak into mine. These people have become lifelong friends of mine—they are family. Go create that team of parents, leaders, and ministers who can change your church and community for Jesus. Go build a great team.

Build relationships with the parents of your kids. They can be a great resource and support for you. Do visitation! Meeting and getting to know families in their own environment (sports, birthday parties, clubs), really shows you care for them and that this is not just a Sunday job for you.

—Becky Garrett, Children's Ministry Leader, Ohio District of the Assemblies of God

Chapter 8

Creating a Safe Place

What a busy morning! Kerri noted with satisfaction that the kids' ministry wasn't just growing in quality and effectiveness; this ministry was just plain growing. It was undeniable. Kerri looked down at the attendance roster in her hands and saw it all there in black in white. Today was another "record" number Sunday in children's church four weeks in a row. This wasn't a fluke or a special-event effect anymore. This was a trend, and they were gaining leaders too. Never as many as she wanted, for sure, but in the past few weeks they had gained several high-capacity, high-impact leaders who were hitting the ground running. The volunteer campaign and subsequent trainings had gone better than expected. That, coupled with all the social media traction they were gaining, was creating a buzz—an excitement that "something" was starting to happen over at First Church. Kerri looked up at the line of parents waiting to pick up their kids now that the service was closing, and she realized that some of these parents had contemplated leaving for the "big church" in the city last year. Were they staying now to check out what was here for their kids? Yikes—no pressure. No pressure. There were also several new faces in that line. What were they thinking? Did they like their first experience here? Did their kids have a great time? "Breathe Kerri, just breathe" she told herself as she squared her shoulders and slapped on her best smile. "We are doing great." She continued her inner pep talk, "Fake it till you make it, Girl." Kerri tried to speed up the quickly forming line by helping check out some of the children. It did seem a little chaotic. The first parent in line seemed impatient and uncertain. She started talking before Kerri could get a word out. "How does this work? Do I just go back and get my child? Where is she? Can I just take her? We have to leave quickly; we have a lunch thing." Kerri jumped to the rescue, "Well, I'll go get her for you! What is her name and grade?" "Sarah Lyman, second grade" "Okay, I'll be right back. No problem." Kerri rounded the hall, still unflustered, humming to herself. She couldn't help but think, are the parents supposed to come back here? How should we be checking the kids out? I know this is the way we have always done it, but we've never had this many kids before. I should give this more thought this week. As Kerri approached the second-grade class, she could hardly hear anything over the loud yelling and squealing. Children were running everywhere and several were crying. She quickly counted at least twenty-two children and one poor frazzled teacher trying to be heard over the noise. It was a little scary.

Kerri shouted, "I need Sarah Lyman, please."

The teacher looked exhausted. "Who?" she shouted back.

"Sarah Lyman—she's new."

The teacher began looking over all the children. While she was distracted, one little boy shoved another smaller boy right over. He started shrieking. Still confused, the teacher looked up at Kerri. "I don't remember. I think I remember seeing a Sarah today. I think she went to the bathroom. But I haven't seen her come back." Kerri blinked several times reflexively. It took a moment to register what she was hearing. Sarah went to the bathroom and didn't come back? By herself? "How long ago did Sarah go to the bathroom?" Kerri asked, struggling to stay calm. "I'm not sure. Ten minutes ago or so? I think?" the teacher responded. Without comment, Kerri turned on her heels and made for the closest bathrooms. Sarah must still be in there, right? Perhaps she just didn't remember how to get back to her classroom. "Sarah?" Kerri called into the ladies' bathroom. "Sarah Lyman? Are you in here?" The silence was deafening. Quickly, Kerri checked each and every stall, with panic growing in her stomach, twisting its way up into her throat. As she made her way back through the hallway, Kerri poked her head into every room and shouted, "Sarah Lyman, are you here?" With each empty classroom, her blood pressure rose.

As she turned the corner back to the parent line, she observed two things right off the bat. (1) Church had definitely let out now, and people were taking their kids seemingly from everywhere. It was very loud and confusing. (2) The parents of Sarah Lyman were now all the way into this hall, their impatience getting the better of them, and right now they were demanding of the frazzled teacher, "Where is our daughter?"

Before Kerri could speak or react, the mother shouted in a high, shrill half-shriek that went ringing down the hallway into the foyer, "YOU LOST MY DAUGHTER? YOU LOST MY SARAH? WHERE IS MY CHILD?" The frantic mother began shouting. Every head of every parent in that line turned to stare at the scene in shock. Then one by one, they each began to panic and run into the kids' areas to find their own child. Kerri stood frozen, stonestill in the hallway, like a rock in a rushing river. None of this seemed real, like an awful nightmare from which she couldn't wake up. This had to be one of the worst moments in her life.

Let's pause here for a second. Whew. Heavy stuff there. Now before you say, "Well, thank you so much for telling such a scary story, Pastor Trisha, just to make a point," I need to tell you: this actually happened at a church where I had just gone on staff (the names have been changed). I really thought the poor children's leader was going to pass out on the floor. She just stood there frozen in shock. My own heart was pounding in my ears as the whole staff, the security team, the leaders, and volunteer parents spread out across the whole building looking for this child. The good news is, this particular story had a happy ending. Eventually we found "Sarah," and she was indeed in *a* bathroom. For reasons unknown, she had gone to a back hallway bathroom that was seldom used and was still "playing" in there. It took some time for the mother to stop crying. But this frightening episode was a blessing in disguise for a few reasons: (1) It demonstrated without a doubt the glaring holes in our security policies and procedures. (2) It was a launching pad for a total rewrite of our policies, which hadn't been reviewed in nine years. At first no one could even tell me where the old policy book even was! (3) The parents, volunteers, and church staff were completely onboard now with tightening and upgrading safety and security. You are really going to need that parent and volunteer buy-in. We'll talk more about that in this chapter. (4) We were blessed that no one was injured or permanently missing in this incident. It was like a quake warning before "the big one," if you will. We used it to spur us to get our act together. (5) It was not the end of our credibility. An incident like this can make it seem impossible to regain the trust of parents and leaders. It isn't impossible. But it is going to be a lot of work. We didn't pretend it didn't happen or sweep it under the rug. We let parents know: We care about your kids, and that is why we are making big changes, starting now. We are doing our homework because we want this to be a safe place for your kids to meet with Jesus and form Christian relationships. Shortly afterward, I called a safety and security forum of leaders, and they showed up. I had their full attention. If you've had "quake warnings," or even if "the big one" hit at your church, don't ignore it, don't make excuses, don't blame, don't defend. Use it as a launching pad to completely change the way that you look at safety and the church.

Now we'll look at the steps that can make your kids' church a safe place.

1. *Check-in and check-out.* This is one of the most basic and important procedures to implement and have running well. Why is it so important?

The child check-in is the first thing that parents see when they come into your church. Parents new to the church are already going to be hesitant to leave their child with you. If you have solid check-in and check-out systems in place, it is very reassuring to parents that you care about the safety of their child. They know that nobody walking in off the street can claim their child. A quality check-in procedure shows care and a commitment for the child's safety right from the start. Did you know, that most people decide in the first ten minutes of entering your church whether they will be back?[12] At that point they haven't even heard your worship team or entered the sanctuary to see all your amazing stage props! They didn't see your drama team, sanctuary

---

[12] Rick Adell, *Must-Know Facts About First-Time Guest (n.d.),* Available at: www.churchleaders.com/pastors/pastor-articles/153325-5-important-facts-about-first-time-guests.html, accessed May 2014

J. Melvin Ming, "Helping Outsiders Become Insiders." (n.d.) J. Melvin Ming. *Enrichment Journal.* Available at: http://enrichmentjournal.ag.org/199903/042_outsiders.cfm. Accessed May 2014

greeters, coffee bar, or hear the message. They've only seen your parking lot team, outer door greeters, and your child check-in team. But they've decided already if they are coming back[13].

Don't you think we should put more preparation and effort into our first impressions? Smart, growing churches take first impressions seriously. And I mean children's ministry first impressions especially. What an opportunity! I always put my best, friendliest people at our check-in desk to put parents and kids at ease. Think about who you have at your doors to the kids' areas. Where do they stand? Are they friendly? Put yourself in the position of a brand new visitor. Would you come back? How can you make your kids' ministry first impressions more inviting, exciting, and reassuring? Do you have the right people in the right positions? This is such a crucial area; take time to think and pray about doing this right. I even created a new volunteer position called the "children's ministries first-impressions coordinator," which includes the greeting, follow-up, and care of new families. I strongly suggest that you, as children's ministry leader, not be the go-to person for this on a Sunday or midweek service. You need to be highly visible, high-fiving kids and kicking off the service. The more you can share the leadership load the better.

---

[13] Bill Emeot, LifeWay Kids' Ministry 101, "First Impressions Mean a Lot", accessed 2014, http://www.lifeway.com/kidsministry/2012/07/31/first-impressions-mean-a-lot/

Making sure kids are where they are supposed to be and that they go home with their own parents is a major safety issue. The main objection I get from to using a standardized check-in and check-out is this: "Well, we've never needed it before, and we already know everybody." We've already covered how much this world has changed in the past decade; heightened security is crucial. A good check-

in/check-out system cuts down on kids roaming around without adult supervision. As far as "we know everyone anyway"—if you never ever have any visitors, there are bigger problems in your church. Why are you not having visitors in your kids' ministry? That is a huge question. If you are growing—which is the idea—then before long you *won't* know everyone there on the weekend.

There is another concern, even if you "already know everyone." Due to my job on the pastoral staff at a church, I am sometimes (not always) aware of which couples are getting divorced or are separated. I know we want to believe that Christians never get divorced, but the reality is that there are Christian families that go through divorce. Even if do know that a couple is getting divorced, I usually do not have a copy of the custody agreement. Are you and all your leaders aware of the custody agreements for each of your families? Maybe not as much as you think. At our church, we once received a disturbing phone call from a dad warning us that his wife did not have custody of the kids anymore and that she was on her way to the church to take the kids. Due to his phone call, the police were waiting when she arrived and she was arrested. But if he hadn't called us, we would have had no idea what was going on. Our rule is *everyone* must check in and out of the kids' ministry at every service, no exceptions. We even have our staff and key volunteers check in and out. A few of them complained that that was not fair because everyone knows who they are. However, I explained that all of our new families do not yet know "who they are," and it seems like favoritism that some people have to check in and out and others don't. It became too complicated to keep track of who had to follow the rules and who didn't, so now everyone must. Of course there will always be parents who lose their claim tickets or keytags or key cards. Our leaders are trained to call me on the radio to manually check the child out, which

How is your relationship w/ Police?

217

includes meeting with the parents and taking down their driver's license numbers before releasing the child to them. I am always cheerful and patient as I explain that their child's safety is our number 1 priority and that we appreciate them helping us out. Most of the time parents are understanding. Usually the biggest resistance comes from long-standing church members who are insulted at having to show a parent tag because "we've been in this church forever." I always thank them for setting a great example for the new families in our growing church. The inconvenience is also a great reminder to remember the tag next time.

There are two types of child check-in methods: paper and electronic. With the paper system, you manually write a number or a first name on the child's sticker and then the same number on the parent's sticker. Most parents do not want you to write their child's full name, address, or phone number on their child's tag, so an assigned number or first name is best. Then you make sure the parent's and child's tags or sticker numbers match at check out. A faster way to do this is to use store bought labels and pre-print two sets of matching random numbers. Try to over estimate how many sets you will need. The drawback is that you will also have to manually write allergies or other concerns onto the label at check-in. It also takes longer to later check the classroom rosters to see who has been missing or who is a visitor, so you can follow up (which you should be doing). This can be time consuming, especially as you grow. It can also be inaccurate because you have to deal with human error in writing down names on the classroom rosters. The benefits of a paper system are that it doesn't cost a lot, doesn't break down as your service is beginning, and it's not affected by power outages, Wi-Fi hiccups, or computer crashes. The paper system is more reliable and easy to understand.

Electronic check-in can be done with a variety of software options and systems. I have used Fellowship One and KidCheck in the past, but there are many others (just Google "church child check-in"). The plusses to an electronic check-in are (A) It ups your credibility and level of excellence in the eyes of your parents, volunteers, and visitors. You look more "official." (B) It's more accurate and detailed. (C) Most important to me, some of these systems have the ability to show you at the push of a button who has been missing more than two weeks, who your visitors were with names and addresses (great for follow-up), your attendance numbers, and so much more. This is gold to children's leaders, pastors, and staff. (D) Some of these systems offer keytags, permanent cards, and free-standing self-check-ins. All of these things speed up your check-in immensely. You'll make your parents, staff, and leaders happy to cut down their wait in line! The drawbacks are: (A) Good programs cost money. Not just for the software, but you need to factor in the touch screens, computers, tablets, cards, labels, keytags, and printers that you will need to run them. You will be buying a lot more than just the software. Make sure you add up the *total* cost. (B) Power outages, Wi-Fi problems, and computer glitches will happen, and you have to be prepared. Churches that use an electronic system must still have a paper backup system available in case of electronic failure. In the last four years, I had this happen three times with one system but twelve times with another. (We ditched the latter one in favor of a more reliable system.) Each time we had to switch to the paper backup. (C) You will need check-in people who can work with a computer system. Your volunteers will need training for what to do if the computer locks up, how to register new people, and what to do if the system goes down. It takes technically minded people, and they will need more training than with the paper system. (D) You will need help and support from people who know the system and who know computers. The system will need periodic upgrades. My husband is an IT guy, so that has given me an advantage. Who at your church will be offering support for your electronic check-in system? You will need it. Whichever system you pick, remember that this is your big opportunity to connect with parents, make a great first impression, and. above all, keep our kids that much safer.

2. *Parent-Call System.* Here is a rule you must understand. It is the "law of the Medes and Persians which altereth not": *The parents are still the primary caregivers for their child, even during your church services.* What does that mean? Well it breaks down into many facets. It means that parents or guardians cannot leave the property during services. We have a policy that we keep posted: "Children in our ministry must have a parent/guardian on the premises during the service. Thank you." The reason we did this was that during our midweek services we had a lot of parents doing a "drop and fly"— dropping kids off for free babysitting then going grocery shopping or out for a date. Why is that such a bad thing? Well, for one thing, it defeats the purpose of getting the whole family into midweek ministry. But more importantly, it sets your church up for trouble if a child is injured. I will never forget one night when a small boy slammed his fingers in a bathroom door. We had an onsite nurse take a look, and she suspected that two of his fingers were broken. When attempting to page his parents, it soon became apparent that they had left the property. After four call attempts, I sat with a crying frightened little boy for over an hour because the hospital refused to treat him without parental

consent. When the parents finally showed up, and we explained the situation, they were very angry at us for not telling them. We showed them that we had called them four times, and they admitted they had turned their phones off for the movie they were watching. For this reason, we began expecting parents to stay somewhere on the grounds during services, whether in a main service, small group, or volunteer area. (Ask them to serve!) This is a family ministry, not a babysitting service. We still have parents who drop and fly, but it's more the exception now instead of the rule. If you have a busing ministry, you will probably need a medical release form, signed by a parent in case of injury, giving you permission to have them treated. I'll accept kids who come to church without parents, but I still always look for a responsible adult to be the contact in case of emergency.

Ask yourself this question: If the need arises to contact a parent during a service, whether for a medical or other reason, how will you get the parent there to pick up their child quickly? It is a mistake to say, "We know everyone, and we'll just go get the parent." If you are growing, and you should be, that method won't work for long. You are also sacrificing one of your volunteers to go through the building in search of the parent. One church I visited brought the screaming child to the parent during the service (after walking around with him through the sanctuary for several minutes). This was distracting for whole congregation. It took too long also for the volunteer to find the parent, and possibly worst of all, I overheard the leader say to the parent, "Here you go. He has a rash spreading all over his body." Everyone within earshot began instinctively scratching. I could only think about how many people were just exposed.

A growing church must have a quick, efficient means of contacting parents during the service. Here are a few of the most popular methods:

a. Sending a teenage or adult runner into the service or around the building and grounds to find the parent. See above for how I feel about this one.

b. Having the pastor or another person on stage announce over the loud speaker: "Mr. Pierce, you need to go pick up your child." Thankfully, I haven't seen this one very often. This is a terrible idea. You may panic or embarrass the parent. It breaks up the flow of the service. It is inefficient and feels sloppy.

c. Putting the parent's or child's name at the bottom of the screen. Again, some parents feel embarrassed and others have complained that they do not want their child's name put out there for potential pedophiles to see. This one hasn't been too popular.

d. Putting the child's tag number (from their check-in sticker) on the screen. I personally like this one. If your church's tech team is willing to work with you, this one may cost little and make a huge difference in how others see the quality of your kids' church. Here's how it works: If a child needs his or her parent, you can text the child's tag number to the sound team to put up on the screen. Another option is: we have an iPad in the kids' area linked to the screen in the main auditorium. I can punch in the child's tag number and it appears at the bottom of the main sanctuary screen until I take it down. Only the person with the matching tag can come back and pick up the child. You will need help from your church's sound team, and you need the pastor or main speaker to let you use a portion of the screen, if necessary.

e. You have probably seen at some churches the red light LED screens on the sides of the sanctuary that show a child's number if a parent needs to pick up the child. The screens are usually connected to a keypad in the children's area. When calling a parent, the children's worker puts in the number and it appears on the screens until the child is picked up. The bonus to this system is that it doesn't take up space on the main screen, and some people find this less distracting than other methods. The drawbacks include much higher costs, and the required installation of new equipment.

All of the above parent-call systems have one major limitation: they only work well in an adult service that is all in one room. Our church has four services and due to space constraints, there are always classes and Bible studies going on in various rooms throughout the building. We also broadcast the service live into other areas of the property. If your church has adults spread throughout your building on Sunday or midweek, then the above systems will be problematic for you, to say the least. Multi-site, multi-space churches usually use one of the following methods to contact parents during a service:

f. Texting or calling a cell phone. I know what you're thinking. "Oh, that's perfect. No equipment to buy, and most people have a cell at church." However, we found that in actual practice, this was a frustrating and mostly useless method for us. The biggest problems were (A) a lot of people put their phones on silent when they enter the service (many churches actually ask you to silence your phone). They do not hear you calling or texting. (B) Usually they give you the mom's phone number, and her phone is deep in her purse. She doesn't feel it vibrate. (C) Some churches do not have good reception in their main sanctuaries for various reasons. The parent may not even get your text until they are leaving. We tried this method, asking parents to please keep their cell phone with them on vibrate—holding parent meetings and handing out reminder postcards. But for our church it just wasn't working. We run a lot of families on Sundays, so we do have times that we need to call parents. Out of the twenty-seven parent calls, I only had parents respond to our texts and calls twice. This method may meet your needs, but it frustrated me enough to go to:

g. A paging system. This is still considered the gold standard for churches and as such is by far the most expensive way to go. How it works is that parents receive a pager for their family when they drop off their kids. They are instructed to keep it on them at all times. Our system has a two-mile radius. When we page a parent the pager lights up all over and vibrates. It is hard to miss, and it doesn't stop until we deactivate it in the kids' area. Another bonus of pagers is you have nothing on the screens that is distracting to the service. Another great feature that I love—if a parent hits the edge of the two-mile radius (like driving away with the pager still in a pocket), an irritating siren goes off and doesn't stop until we deactivate it. I'll admit this feature has been a bit hilarious to me when parents have tried sneaking off property to shop or go to dinner. They sheepishly return to have us deactivate it before it drives them insane. This keeps us from losing a lot of very expensive pagers too. The biggest drawback to this one is its cost.

Bottom line: you must have a way to contact parents during a service. A lot of what you need depends on, and changes with, the size and layout of your church. This may even take some trial and error. But find what works best for you!

3. *Entrances and exits.* How many entrances and exits does your kids' area have? Where are they? It is a good idea to print out a map of the area and look at where people can enter and leave. Where are the areas of highest traffic, and where is it bottle-necking? Your parents will get frustrated and irritated if they have to wait in long lines to check in and out, squeezing through congested areas, not knowing where to go. Most importantly, you need to make it as difficult as possible for someone to slip in a back door, grab a child, and leave unnoticed. Remember: your church may be open to all people, but your kids' area should not. Here are a few tips for securing your entrances and exits:

A. The fewer entrances and exits in the kid's area the better. Having too many exits is just asking for a child to wander off somewhere or the wrong person to walk in. You probably do not have enough volunteers to man every door. You must keep your fire exits unblocked at all times. But how

many other doors don't need to be used? Which could become entrance only or exit only?

B. Make it clear which way people need to go. I love getting movie theater type stanchions and creatively roping off areas to help direct the flow of traffic, especially around the check-in and check-out area. Go overboard with professionally made signage so people know exactly where to find the "elementary entrance," or the "preschool pickup." The more prep work you do, the clearer your directions, the smoother your check-in and check-out will proceed, eliminating so much frustration.

C. Consider making the nearest outdoor entrance to the kids' area a "family check-in entrance," and mark it well in the parking lot.

D. Consider getting those loud obnoxious alarms (I got mine at the hardware store) for some of your outer doors, so that if a child does wander out, everyone will know.

E. Decide which bathrooms the kids will use. I suggest kids never go alone to some out-of-the-way back bathroom. Can you somehow make a kids' only bathroom area? Remember that from elementary up, adult and teenage leaders should not go into the bathroom with a child but should wait just outside until the child is finished.

F. Which outer doors need to be locked so people cannot walk into the kids' areas? It will not kill anyone to walk around to another door. The safety of the kids has priority over adults being inconvenienced.

4. *Tight screening*. Background checks are not optional anymore. If you put a sex offender in a kids' classroom without having done a background check, the church will probably be sued, and rightly so.

I once saw an interview with a convicted child rapist who said, "They are right to keep me locked up. If they let me out, I will do it again. And we just go straight to churches. They don't check. They let us right in. They're trusting." I was sickened. Vomited in my mouth a little. He described going around to different churches and targeting the one that had the fewest systems in place to protect the kids. This reminded me of a predator casing a wildebeest herd, looking for the smallest, weakest, or sickest animal to prey on.

What a poor job we have done at times protecting our kids. The program I was watching went on to say that many sex offenders consider churches to be "soft targets" that are easy to enter. We must change this no matter what it costs. How can we claim to love children in Jesus Name and still fail to do even the minimum to protect them. We shouldn't need to catch up to the rest of the world; we should be setting the standard. Let's look at sensible steps to screen out predators.

A. Fingerprinting and background checks. Your first line of defense is a full background check. No one should be working in your kids' areas without completing one. Background checks do not catch everything, but they tell you a lot. I have heard the debate over whether you just need the state-level check or if you should go for federal too. I vote federal. The more thorough the better. A state background check will only catch offenses that occurred in your state, and to me that's not enough. The cost can be prohibitive to some churches, but it is important enough to find a way. Some larger churches ask volunteers to pay part or all of the screening cost. Also find out where you can send your volunteers for fingerprinting. Our church invested in a fingerprinting computer so we can do this onsite.

B. A volunteer application. You also need a well-written application. You can find examples online, and I suggest looking over several before writing your own.

C. Check references. Make sure to get references, talk to previous pastors, and drill down on anything that doesn't "look right" on that application.

D. Meet in person. We meet and talk to all of our volunteers personally before placing them somewhere. Your kids' ministry screening should be the most stringent in the entire church, because these are our kids. Don't apologize for it. It is better to leave a position open than to fill it with a potentially dangerous person. Again, listen to your gut (i.e., the Holy Spirit).

E. Allow no exceptions. Screen everyone. You usually cannot check teens under age eighteen, but all adult men and women need to be screened. You even need to screen the ones who are in place when you start your position if they've never been checked. Innocent people shouldn't need to get defensive about this; it's about keeping our kids safe. For this to work, it has to be across the board. It will hurt your credibility if it gets out that you made exceptions for people you like or who have clout.

F. Shadow a new leader for a time. If the background check comes back clean, and the references check out, and things are looking and feeling right, start the person off with an experienced teacher for training (shadowing). *Follow the rule of three: Always have a minimum of three adults in a room. No adult can ever be alone with a child.*

G. Ongoing trainings. This tight screening protects the kids, and it protects your leaders, and it protects you. I suggest you and your leaders obtain more information on further training and keep up with updates. I am not personally endorsing the following, but here are a few websites to get you started: www.churchmutual.com,

www.churchstaffing.com, www.safechurch.com (guideone), and www.protectmyministry.com.

5. *Allergies and food intolerances.* Here is another area that has changed dramatically in the last few years. When I was a kid, everyone

ate peanut butter and jelly sandwiches at school nearly every day, especially on meatloaf day.

In 2013, many schools in Ohio banned all peanut products from their lunchrooms due to peanut allergies. Like a lot of children's pastors, it took a few close calls to wake me up and make me take this more seriously. So please learn from my mistakes. First off, one of my most dedicated teachers brought her daughter with her one day and the little girl had a terrible reaction with hives that began to close off her throat. We had to use her EpiPen and it was frightening. All because she was close to a boy who had just eaten a peanut butter sandwich and had "peanut breath." Secondly, an elementary teacher brought in icecream treats for the whole class, some of which had peanut topping. One child had to leave the room for the duration of the class. Another Sunday, an eleven-year-old boy collapsed hitting his head and went into a severe diabetic reaction after eating a candy bar his teacher handed out. I met with our parent board, and the other staff, and we decided together to make our kids' areas peanut free. We looked at all of the snacks we were giving out. I really want to make sure all children can come enjoy kids' church, even if we have to skip the peanut topping. We've posted "peanut free" signs throughout our area and sent out communications to parents and leaders. We now special-order all of our nursery and pre-K snacks in bulk from a factory that sells "peanut-free" products—pretzels, goldfish and raisins (for the kids who are gluten free), and all of these are also free of citrus, dairy, egg, shellfish and red dye. We also post our list of snacks for parents to see. Our check-in system prints out a child's food allergies on their tag in red so the teacher is aware. As difficult as this sounds, it has freed us up to concentrate on our services and not worry (as much) about a child missing out due to a reaction. The focus shouldn't be on snacks anyway; our focus is connecting kids with God. Anything that might distract from that needs to go. Even the Red dye 40.

6. *Medications.* The best rule about giving medications to kids is don't. A church is not a school. You and the church can get in a lot of trouble for giving a child or adolescent medication for any reason. You probably do not have a signed parent consent form on file to dispense medications. And if a parent requests that you do so, do you want to make your volunteers responsible for administering the right dosage and on time? We only have the children about an hour. My leaders, volunteers, and I do not give any medications during that time. If a parent feels it is necessary, we have the parent return and give medications to their own child. This ban on giving medications even includes over-the-counter medications including Tylenol, aspirin,

Pepto-Bismol, and so on. You should never give medication to a minor unless it is your own child. If the need arises, call the parent. Along these lines, please go through any first-aid kits you may have in your classrooms and remove the medications. Even antibiotic ointment is not allowed (some children have allergies to it). Don't leave medications in the classrooms and risk that someone may use them. The only treatments we are allowed to provide are ice packs and Band-Aids. And we still write an incident report (sample at the back of this book) and notify the parent. Our rule is parents give medications to their own child. No exceptions.

Did you know that hand sanitizer, which is now a very popular item in many public places including churches, can be very dangerous for children? Hand sanitizer is made almost entirely of alcohol. And what do little children, especially those in pre-K and toddlers, do with their fingers a lot? They put them in their mouth! And even a very small amount of hand sanitizer can get a small child intoxicated, sick, or lead to more serious consequences. Several churches have reported disastrous consequences of children ingesting hand sanitizer during services and being given back to their parents intoxicated or needing to be hospitalized. Please go through your classrooms and put hand sanitizer up high. Insist that your teachers keep it as high up as possible. Children should not be allowed to dispense it themselves. Only small amounts are needed, and your teachers and leaders must be trained about the dangers of leaving any chemical in reach of a child.

7. *Well-child policy.* Common sense tells us that when your child is vomiting, has a fever, or is blowing lots of thick green guk out his nose, you stay home with him until he is well. Your work would not be happy with you if you brought that child with you into the office and held him on your lap hacking stuff up during a meeting. And the schools all have "well-child" policies that would keep you from leaving your child in class that day puking in a bucket under his desk or passing out during gym. Doctor's offices would make your child with a heavy cough wear a mask while there. So why do we treat church so differently? I overheard a staff member whispering to another staff member once, "I would never ever leave my child in the nursery here. That place is a Petri dish of every bacteria known to man. No one leaves there healthy!" Several parents responded to our survey saying they wouldn't use the nursery for fear of their child catching an illness. It was time to act. We researched well-child policies from surrounding schools and churches and came up with our own that matches our needs. At first we caught a lot of backlash. I had the volunteers call me over to speak with parents who were not being able to leave a sick

child. I got a lot of excuses like "Well, the school won't take him either and I really need a break. Here you take him!" And "Oh yeah, that rash has been spreading all over his legs since this morning. He caught it at daycare, but it's not contagious." and "This is a church. You have to take anyone!" No wonder people didn't want to use the nursery. Again, I didn't understand this until I had kids of my own and found out that one nasty virus could waylay our whole family for a week. The bottom line is that you need to do your research, come up with a solid well-child policy, and have your pastor approve it. Then you need to post it somewhere visible so you can make it apparent you are not targeting any particular child; this is the policy across the board. It is extremely important to make sure no parent feels singled out or embarrassed in front of others. Yes you do have to turn some children away if they are too ill, for the safety of all the other children and your workers, but remember to be kind and caring. That poor parent may have had a very rough week and thought "maybe we are well enough now to finally get out" when they just weren't quite ready. Always use grace and kindness. But keep that kids' area a "well-child area" as much as you possibly can.

8. Unattended children. This is becoming more of a hot topic among children's leaders. Let me try to frame the dilemma. Each Sunday and

midweek you have many volunteers coming to church early—parking lot teams, cafe teams, greeters, worship team, sound team, kids' ministry volunteers and more. For some churches, this hour to two hours before the service begins is "free time" for children to run all over the church unsupervised. This has led to children getting injured, and the churches being sued for negligence (because they still were injured on your property). Even if an outside group rents your church and lets kids run unsupervised and a child gets hurt (and kids do get hurt sometimes) the parents can go after the church's insurance money because it happened on your property. A less severe consequence of unsupervised children roaming the building is that many times the snacks and food go missing, equipment is broken, and supplies are used up that were needed for church services. And then when the church service begins, someone has to go find all of these roaming children to bring them over to be checked in. My bottom line is that unsupervised children roaming the building is a bad idea. No good can come of that. And if you allow certain kids to run wild (staff or key volunteer kids), you will either have to allow this for all or prepare your standard answer for when a parent calls "favoritism" and "unfair." I do understand this, because my own children have to be at church early with me when I'm setting up. I just make sure my kids stay with me and help with set up. So what is the answer for the parents who volunteer? That is a tricky question that is causing heated debates in more than one church. Some have suggested, "We need the volunteers here, and since kids are involved, the children's ministry volunteers must provide child care or start their programs an hour or more early." This goes right back to the whole babysitting versus children's ministry debate. This is an issue we are still working through. As you probably know, it is hard enough to get your volunteers there by fifteen minutes early, much less an hour. Your curriculum will not cover two to three hours. And I have never wanted my children's ministry leaders thinking that I recruited them to babysit. We keep our doors shut completely until twenty minutes before a service starts. When we open our doors, there is already worship and other activities going on for the kids. And from the time our doors open until parent check-out, kids are never unattended or left with "free time." Our volunteers who come early to set up keep their kids with them and usually have their kids help. Other departments have gotten creative; the worship team hires a babysitter to watch the children of the worship leaders who are required to be there two hours before every service. Door greeters who arrive 40 minutes early have been having their children help them set up, or they have a teenager watch their children until our check-in opens. Regardless of what your church decides to do, it is imperative that you address the issue of unattended children at church.

9. Professional assessment. The best decision you can make in regards to safety and security is to invest in a professional opinion. There is a wide range of options and prices out there. A good place to start would be to ask your local fire chief or police chief to go through your areas and provide suggestions. If you have a police officer or security manager in your church, they may be a good resource. Have a school teacher or a daycare professional keep you up to date on changes in child-safety policies. A security professional went through our kids' areas with a fine-tooth comb and then gave me a written list of recommendations specific to our situation. This was a useful tool when I proposed changes in our safety procedures to our parent team, the church board, and the other staff. A written, personalized recommendation will cost you, but it may be worth it for your church. Why do you need an outside, experienced voice in this area? Well for one, fire safety is not something you should be guessing about, especially when children are involved. I am not a fire fighter, so when we began planning our fire evacuation plan, our fire department graciously helped  us out! When you are planning what to do in the event of a tornado,

live shooter, or a medical emergency, collaborate with your local police and emergency teams so that your plan works with local laws and procedures. We had a security expert in our own congregation and he was a great collaborator and contributor when writing our policies and procedures! Don't guess; include the people who know.

10. *Weather, medical, and violence emergencies.* The time to plan for an emergency is not when the tornado siren goes off. Do your pre-K teachers know what to do in the event of a power outage? What if one of your second graders suddenly has a seizure? Can you quickly get in contact with the parent? Who calls 911? Who holds the doors and directs the medical team? Who takes care of the other kids? Here's a little known fact: Please don't laugh, but a long time ago in a galaxy far, far away, I used to be a security officer in downtown Minneapolis. I did recruitment and the trainings for our officers. One of the points I made to all of my new officers was this: "What will you do in case of an emergency? You will do exactly what you have practiced. You will do only what you were trained to do."

Most of us are the same way. In a serious or dangerous situation, you will do what you know, what you have rehearsed, and what you are trained to do. Unfortunately, for many of our volunteer kid's leaders, when an emergency happens, they will do exactly what they have rehearsed and have trained to do—which is absolutely nothing. Some will stand and stare in shock, their brains spinning, searching in vain for a memory of what they need to do now. The time to decide on a plan and do your trainings is now, before an incident happens. It is very important that this doesn't become a "once-and-done" topic. Your team will need ongoing trainings and reminders about your policies and procedures. Your written policies will need to be looked at periodically (I suggest at least every two years). Here are a few tips to getting a plan and trainings going for weather, medical, and violence emergencies:

A. Decide now what you need to do in the event of a tornado, fire, flood, earthquake, violent event, or power outage). Seek help from experts while devising your policies. The hard part is coming up with the plan, writing it down, and doing the initial training. But it is crucial and so worth it.

B. Work with the leadership of your church to coordinate all of your efforts. Be careful about what is said to parents from the pulpit. Just imagine you are a parent sitting in the worship service and you hear the pastor say, "Oh, hey, a child was just seriously injured in the kids' area and needs an ambulance. Let's all stop and pray." If you were a parent in that room, what would you do? You'd run straight over there in a panic to make sure your child is okay. You have to be careful saying "fire, violent incident, lost child, injured child" from the pulpit. I cannot stress enough how important it is for staff to cooperate in creating a church-wide plan for working together in an emergency.

C. In the event of a serious weather, medical, fire, or violent emergency, it is crucial that you have good classroom rosters of which kids are in which class and check off that each child is there. If parents catch wind of the event, they may panic, run to the kids' area, grab their child, and run. You cannot let this happen until you have completed a headcount. As parents, it is our nature (mine included) to run over and make sure our child is okay, snatch them up, and run home. But if there is a fire in the building and you haven't done a headcount, you may not remember the names of every child who was in your class that day. And when parents are grabbing kids left and right, we have no idea which kids got out and which are still in the burning building. It could result in sending fire fighters, police officers, or medical personnel into a very dangerous, life-threatening situation, searching for a child who already went home. Keep your head and ask parents to hang on a moment while you cross off their child's name on the roster. Keep order as best you can no matter the situation. *Have your leaders*

continue to keep track of who was checked out by a parent and when.
That's hard to do in an emergency, but very important nonetheless.

D. Share this load. The safety of the kids is the whole church's job.
You need to formulate plans and trainings alongside your security
team, leadership staff, and parent advisory board. My parent board was
amazing in coming up with ideas and helping me gain the buy in of the
congregation as a whole. Communicate your plan freely with parents,
leaders, and staff. Post it in various places, if you can.

11. *Facility dangers.* Many times a new or different set of eyes comes
in very handy. Facility dangers include problems with furniture, the
building, or church equipment that could pose a danger to a child. Why
do you think it is so beneficial to have someone new do a walk through
with you to identify potential problems with the facility? The reality is
that unless you are new to the church, you may be walking right past
things in the hallways or classrooms every week and not really notice
what is there. You can see without seeing. This is not your fault and not
entirely in your control. Studies have proven that after six months of
being in a new job, new building, or new area your brain no longer
considers the information it is receiving about the environment as new.
Your heightened senses go into autopilot so your brain can focus on
other "new" information in your life. The American Psychological

Association calls this "automatic cognitive processing."

behind the kids' stage that bothered you so much your first week,

isn't even on your radar anymore. Then a new parent or an intern visits

and says, "Wow, what's with all the candy wrappers behind the puppet

stage?" And your first thought is, "How long has that been there? Or "I

forgot about that." Your brain is preprogrammed to begin glossing over

visual information so it can pay attention to newer information. Have

you ever taken your usual drive to work and not really remembered all

of it when you got there? As scary as that may seem, that is how your

brain uses its "autopilot" on old information, so that it can to focus on

other things. The longer you have been at the church, the worse your

perspective can become. Have a fire fighter, daycare supervisor, or

security specialist walk through your kids' area periodically to check

for issues with safety.

Now we are going to do a little field trip. With someone of your choice,

walk through your kids' areas and answer the following questions. And

be honest! Jesus is watching.

Are your fire exits all completely clear?   Y or N

Are your hallways free of clutter and old junk? It is dangerous, sloppy,

and a fire hazard to use your hallway for storage. (I know how badly

we all need more storage)   Y or N

Could a child pull something down on themselves? A good rule here is that if they can, they will. Y or N

Are all your TVs and heavy equipment bolted to the wall? Are your shelves anchored? Y or N

Are there jagged edges on or under your tables (kids crawl under there, let's just be honest)? Y or N

Are there splinters or jagged edges on your door frames? Y or N

Lead paint chips? Exposed wiring? Y or N

Are cords taped down or up high? Cords pose a nasty tripping hazard.

Y or N

Are there toys in the nursery that are broken, choking hazards, or fragile? Y or N

Are the rooms and toys disinfected regularly? Y or N

Are all chemicals, paints, cleaning supplies, insecticides, or other toxic supplies moved out of the kid's areas and secured? Y or N

Are there too many things plugged into one socket? Y or N
(Too many things plugged into one socket started a fire in our church library once.)

So how do you think your church did on your facility safety check? Give it a grade _____

What area needs the most immediate attention and corrections?

_____

_____

_____

Here's a tip: We have a checklist posted on the wall of each classroom listing what the leaders need to do and check each week before they leave. It doesn't take long and it keeps safety in the forefront of our minds. I ask them to test their radio and check the battery level, dispose of all trash and broken toys, report anything missing from the first aid kit, and report any broken equipment, including tables and chairs.

12. *Essential weekly safety supplies.* What safety supplies do you need each week? Make sure you get these as soon as possible:

a. Incident report forms: If you haven't yet had a medical incident, injury, or a child reporting guardian abuse, you will. When I was working in security, we had a rule: when it comes to the law and court cases, if it is not in writing, it did not happen. In other words, you need to actually document what happened—who, what, where, when, and why—while it is still fresh in everyone's minds. Soon after the fact, memories of the event start to fade and are less reliable. Not sure whether you should write up an incident report? If in doubt, write it out. Take some time and look at several other church's incident reports (your church may already have one that they may or may not be using). See an example of the one I currently use in the back of this book. Make sure you have one available every week in the kids' area and use it any time there is an injury, emergency, or dangerous incident. Then make a copy of it, give it to your pastor right away, and file the original. The next time the need arises, you will be thanking God you kept a written record. Train your leaders to fill one out for any and all incidents and injuries. You won't be sorry you did.

b. Medical kits. I keep a well-marked first aid kit mounted on the wall in every classroom. It has Band-Aids and gauze but no medications or creams.

c. Radios. Your leaders need a way to communicate with you, staff, and security. Radios are a great investment. Make sure to have training on how to use them properly and keep them charged.

d. Flashlights. These are so important in the event of a power outage. I suggest two per classroom. I prefer the LED shake lights that almost never need a battery change.

e. Class roster. Have your teachers write down who is in every class at every service. It only takes a moment at the start of service. As we talked about before, this roster is pure gold if there is an emergency, and you need to make sure every child is out safely.

f. Fire alarms and fire extinguishers. Make sure all your leaders know where these are and how to use them. But remind them the priority is on getting the kids out, and calling for help-not fighting fires.

g. Policies and procedures page. This is the condensed policies and procedures statement you need to create and post in every classroom. Make sure it includes your church's emergency plans and evacuation routes. During a visit to a public school, I saw their procedures posted in the document shown in the photo on this page. This is a good model for a document to post by the phones and in each classroom. Honestly, in the event of an emergency, who is actually going to stop and say, "Hang on. What was I supposed to do if a child has a seizure? It is on pages 204 and 205 in the big manual.

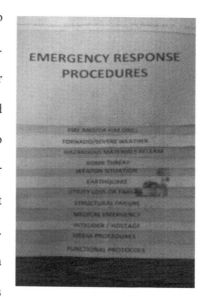

[flipping pages] Oh no, it's actually back on page 115 under medical emergencies." That just won't work. In the event of an actual emergency, your leaders will revert to what they were trained to do, and they may look at a posted procedure on the wall. Your shortened procedures page that is posted on the wall needs to include the following:

* In the event of any emergency, call 911. If in doubt, call 911. Tell the dispatcher which door the responders should enter to be closer to the emergency

* Call on your radio to your area leader right after you call 911.

* Notify leadership staff and security

* Send an adult to direct the emergency teams, who will not know the layout of your building.

* If a child is in danger, do what you can to help, but do not leave the other children unattended.

* Do not let children run out without being checked off the roster.

* When the incident is over, fill out an incident form found _____ and return it to _____ before leaving today. Thank you!

Safety and security in children's ministry may not be the most cheerful and exciting part of children's ministry. It's not necessarily what you

thought of when you said yes to being a kids' leader. This is a "living" part of your kids' ministry that grows and changes. Children's ministry safety and security is never "done"; it is ongoing. Laws vary from state to state and change constantly, and you need to be on top of those changes. What cannot change is how much we work to protect the children in our churches. Let's pray hard and do all we can to create and maintain a safe place, where all kids can experience the life-changing love of God.

Chapter 9

The Illustrative Methods

Get the Upgrades

Every eye is riveted on the man on stage in the shiny sequin outfit. He has the full attention of every child, parent, and leader in the room. No one dares breathe as he pushes off with his unicycle out onto the tight rope. He wobbles once and the crowd gasps. But as he rights himself, the laser show begins, and the smoke and fog come on. The music is pumping and vibrating all along the floor. Just when you think this cannot get any more intense, he pulls out the flaming torches and begins to juggle not one, or two, but six of them one handed! The crowd bursts into thunderous applause, but he's not done yet. With his other hand he pulls out a puppet and begins the funniest ventriloquist act anyone has ever seen. Right below him, his wife is doing black light chalk art while leading a dynamic kids' worship team. For a grand finale, the man back flips off the tightrope down to the stage. Wow, did he stick that landing! He catches the puppet, the unicycle, all six torches (still on fire), takes a bow, and says with a flourish, "And that, kids, is why we can trust that God made the world. Let's close in prayer."

Now back to reality (though that would be a stinkin' wild kids' church, wouldn't it?). What I just described may sound absurd, but unfortunately, this is what some leaders think of when they hear the term *children's pastor*. They immediately think of a special speaker at a camp they went to, or someone on a kids' show they saw once, and they are intimidated. They think "I can never be *that*."

As we covered in the previous chapters, chances are, your church is not going to get a former Ringling Brothers kids' pastor. God didn't send them Siegfried or Roy. God sent them you. Don't feel qualified? Then you are in good company, with the likes of Gideon, Jeremiah, Moses, Isaiah, and many others. You don't need to be a rock star to make an eternal impact on the kids He entrusted to you. You need to be faithful, real, and you need to love (kids can spot a fake). God uses and blesses faithful people, not perfect people.

Having said that, in this chapter, I am going to ask you to open up to exciting possibilities that I call (drum roll, please) the illustrative methods. Illustrative methods are creative ways of illustrating your message and ordering your service. They include object lessons, puppetry, dance, and so on. It does not take the place of the message, but it serves the message by bringing it to life.

Isn't it annoying when you purchase something only to discover you only bought the basic form of it? And all the really fun stuff is "extra" or "upgrades"? Well, your curriculums are your basic package, and the illustrative methods are the upgrades. So we are about to explore the different illustrative methods and how they can take your kids' services to a whole new level.

But first let's look at a more fundamental question: Why use illustrative methods at all? If you have a curriculum, why not be safe and read out of the book?

Good question. Imagine you are out to dinner with friends. You are very hungry and excited to taste this new restaurant's food. The decor is all brand new and amazing. When the waiter comes to your table, before you can even order, he uses a can opener to open a can of generic SpaghettiOs, which he unceremoniously dumps out onto your plate cold. Then he hands you a spoon. You realize everyone in the restaurant is handed the same thing. Would you be happy? Would you go back? If you were served a premade, prepackaged dish that took no thought, creativity or effort, wouldn't you think, "They are capable of so much more"?

Now imagine that you are again out to dinner with friends, and you are once again very hungry. The decor is not quite so nice this time. It's older, like a ma and pa type of thing. The waiter is attentive, and the menu shows that someone here was intentionally working to offer what this community was hungry for. Within minutes of arriving you are treated to several different courses of hot, fresh, flavorful food that hits the spot. You didn't know what to expect next, but you were excited to find out. It met the needs you had at that time. The restaurant exceeded your expectations with quality, excellence, and service. And you couldn't wait to come back again for more-and bring even more of your friends.

Which of these scenarios is closer to how you are currently preparing your kids' church service? As children enter our areas on Sunday morning, do we open the "can" of curriculum, serve it up cold, say a prayer, and go home? Or do we use the curriculum as a plate on which to build an amazing service? Do we craft a service that intentionally addresses the unique needs of this group of kids? Is it done with creative visual and kinesthetic elements to reach all of our kids? Cookie cutter just won't get it done. I'm not talking chocolate pudding mudslides on your first week. My point is we are capable of so much more.

How much more could we be doing with our services? At times, we all long to get to do what those "other children's leaders" do. We marvel at some childrens' pastor's success and innovation. Tell me- what would you do in your kid's church services right now if money were no object, if you could do anything and be assured of success? Write out what your kid's church services could look like in your wildest dreams:

_____

_____

_____

_____

Think carefully with me for a moment. How many of these elements could you get started on now? I believe that it is not our building restraints or our budget restraints holding us back. The most important elements for growth are not really high tech equipment, the latest curriculum or the brightest wall colors. What we desperately need is faith, creativity, innovation, and manpower (or woman power). And some of your greatest tools for crafting that kid's service you dream of are: *the illustrative methods.*

In what ways could your church benefit from using creative kid's service elements?

A. If you incorporate the illustrative methods- you'll have more effective, higher quality services. Most if not all of the creative service methods I am about to share with you require little or no money to do, but they will bump your service's quality up exponentially. Your service's excellence level will go through the roof. Once you start implementing creative ministry methods in your kids' ministry—

strategically crafting your services and gaining a team—your services will jump to a whole new level. Everyone will start to feel the excitement when they see what is possible. People will start dreaming of even better things you can try. Word will get around that this group is aiming for high quality.

B. If you incorporate the illustrative methods- you'll meet more of the needs of your specific group of kids. People must always trump programming. I tell our teachers, that if a child comes in with a need, then you stop to show love and pray for that child. I don't care if we get to the end of the curriculum for that day, as long as we prayed with that child whose parents are going through a divorce. Kids are coming in with more needs and heartache than I've ever seen before. Some have suffered more in their few young years than I've seen in all of mine. This is not the same world in which we adults grew up.

Can you describe your demographic—your group of kids—in detail? This may take some contemplating and asking questions. Are most of your kids' parents married? Are the majority middle class, upper class, or are they facing poverty? Did a lot of their parents lose jobs this year? What is the racial demographic in your church? In your community? What are these kids really into—TV shows? Movies? Which books? What games? What school activities? What sports?

What is the greatest challenge they face week to week? You need to know these things to adequately speak into their lives, especially if you didn't grow up in the region.

When Paul entered a new community, notice that he always spoke the language and followed the customs of the people there. He said, "I am all things to all men, that by all means I might save some" (1 Corinthians 9:22). Do we have that attitude when it comes to our kids in the church? If we do not learn their culture, which can be far different from our own, we are not speaking their language. Imagine if I were going to be a missionary in China. After doing all the work to go to China, I start screaming at the people in Swahili. Should I be surprised or angry at my audience for squirming and not paying attention? In China you need to speak Chinese (and the right dialect, for that matter). As a children's leader, you must speak "the language" and the "dialect" of your group of kids if you hope to be effective. Did I particularly want to go watch *High School Musical*? No, but I went because my entire kids' church was talking about it. And it was an eye opener. I even incorporated illustrations on it into our programs, and, believe me, we had their full attention.

In the lines below, describe the children in your church. What are their likes and dislikes? Races? Activities? Sports? Be as detailed as possible:

_____

_____

_____

_____

Thinking about these kids as people whom God loves and for whom Jesus died, and who have specific needs, what messages would speak to them the most? What would get their full attention? How can you craft your entire kids' service to reach these kids (and their families)? It may be the most important question you can ask in kids' ministry.

C. If you incorporate the illustrative methods- you'll involve and retain more families by allowing them to serve. Using more illustrative methods involves more people in this ministry, including involving the kids in their own ministry! A church can be great at bringing new people in, but poor at retaining those new families. The best way I have found to keep those new people is to involve them. When you involve others in the ministry, you help them understand and use their own unique gifts from God. You give them a safe place to make mistakes, grow, learn, and lead. If you do not currently have opportunities for kids and families to serve in your kids' church, then the time has come to create those opportunities. The illustrative methods are the best way I know to include a wide range of people of all ages in their ministry. These kids are aching to help and serve. They lead on their sports teams, and speech teams, and music teams at school. Let's not make church the only place they have to just sit and listen. Bottom line: we will keep the ones we include and who find their niche.

D. If you incorporate the illustrative methods-you'll minister to a wider range of children, with all different learning styles. Long gone are the days of standing up front, reading out of a book, while all the children sit passively. You've heard the old adage, "We remember only 20 percent of what we hear, 40 percent of what we see, 62 percent of what we see and hear, and 80 percent of what we do"? That's even more incentive to involve these kids in serving in church. If you stand and read a lesson to the kids every week, you are using the lowest form and least effective means of communicating to kids. Last I checked, the Bible said that God was not willing that any should perish but that all should come to repentance. (2 Peter 3:9) That includes the kids in your church each week who are mainly visual learners. The auditory reading is not getting through to them. Do we have that time to waste? No way. What about your kids who are kinesthetic learners and learn best by doing, like acting it out, making something, or doing a puppet skit? Kids are more visual and kinesthetic learners than ever before. I happen to be a highly visual learner, and I do tend to zone out in a long lecture. One study found that more boys than girls were visual or kinesthetic learners. Do you have boys who struggle to sit still in kids' church and don't seem to get the point? What about the rise in children with ADHD and highly intelligent or gifted kids? They do better with visual or kinesthetic learning (give them something to do). No matter what, these are kids for whom Christ died. These are kids He loves dearly, and he put them in your class. Instead of getting frustrated with the kids and hammering them to change, let's be the adults here and get creative. It's not the message that needs to change; just the methods. Let's take the central theme of the Sunday and break it down so that every child goes home "getting it." The illustrative methods are the best way I know to reach the largest number of kids.

E. If you incorporate the illustrative methods- you'll grow numerically. Though sheer numbers are not the goal, when you include others in the ministry, when you include all learning types, your numbers will go up. It's just a fact and a byproduct of being intentional. It's kind of like taking your time crafting a delicious meal (there's that metaphor again). It shouldn't be a shock to anyone that it tastes so much better and attracts more people than a cold lunchable. Many times the rule applies, "You will get what you plan for." If you plan nothing, you will get nothing. If you want to grow and thrive, you have to plan to grow and thrive.

Also, remember what we said about the "child-driven household"? American families are run by the needs, wants, and desires of the child. I am not condoning that lifestyle, but this is another time that you can use culture to reach people. There are people in your community who won't set foot in a church at all. There are people who are far from God, who are atheists, alcoholics, addicts, or just plain mad at God. They will not come to your church for your pastor's sermon, your outreach dinner, your picnic, your coffee bar, your free mug day, your awesome worship team or your prayer service.

But they will come to hear their granddaughter sing.

I found out long ago that whenever I did a kids' talent night, parents I had never met, who told me flat out they would never go to church, were suddenly coming out of the woodwork to see their kids minister. When our kids did a Christmas outreach with dance and drama, everyone came. The parents, the grandparents, the aunt and uncles, and mom's second cousin's roommate's younger brother. If you want to reach whole families for Jesus, then let the kids serve. Let them lead in their gifts.

Need another reason? Parents will make sure they get those kids to church if their child is doing something in the service that day. Remember how the average American family only goes to church one or two times a month? Well, if their child is scheduled to be in a drama that morning, and people are counting on them, and that child cannot wait to go on, then more than likely that parent will not hit the snooze, roll over and skip that Sunday.

Every church that I've seen institute kids in ministry through illustrative methods has had a jump in attendance. It's no coincidence. Once a parent pulled me aside on a Sunday morning. She was frazzled, irritated, and looked exhausted. She said, "Well, I hope you're happy, Pastor Trish. All my kid wants to do now is be at church for every service every Sunday. This is all your fault for letting him help in the sound booth. We forgot he was on this Sunday, so last night we had to leave our vacation two days early and drive all night long just to get here in time. This church stuff has gotten out of hand, but he loves it so now we're stuck. We have to do it."

She was frustrated. But inside I was rejoicing that this kid was running his whole family, that this boy who once hated church now wants to live here, and that this poor mom was ready to beat me over it. I didn't have the heart to tell her that her son wasn't even scheduled that day. He thought he was, but the parents didn't look at the schedules I sent out. (I am careful to never over schedule someone. Kids will try to do it all every week.)

Remember, if you use illustrative methods in ministry, your kids will bring their friends to watch. You will gain kids, parents, and new leaders who love being a part of something exciting and growing.

F. If you incorporate illustrative methods- you'll soon open new doors of ministry and outreach in your community. Do you dream of your church having a greater voice in the schools (public, Christian, and private) in your region? Do you wish your church could reach unchurched kids in the neighboring apartment complexes? What if your kids' church could impact hundreds of people at your local mall? What about sharing the love of Christ at a veterans' center or hospital or nursing home or juvenile hall? The truth is I have been honored to do all of the above with our kids' church service teams, not because they wanted us to come in and play a video or read a lesson. We were asked to come in because of interest in the creative ideas we were using— kids' choir, puppetry, juggling, dance teams, kids' doing artwork and making cards, and more. As the Bible says, "Your gift will make a way for you, even into the presence of kings" (Proverbs 18:16).

When I was doing kids' ministry in Africa one summer, this Scripture became literally true right in front of our eyes! The teen challenge center we were working with has a youth choir that sings and dances. It is amazing to watch these young people, many of them orphaned by AIDS, leading worship with such profound joy. One week, they told me they had just received word that the nation's top leaders had requested a personal concert for them and their families. They were naturally extremely nervous and asked for special prayer over them as they ministered. Their gift and dedication made a way for them to minister in beyond their wildest dreams.

Conduct your ministry with excellence and it will open doors of ministry all around you to people who need Jesus. Start thinking now about upcoming events in which your team could participate. Start small. I started one puppet and dance team with a craft-store grand opening.

266

When they got more experience, we did a twenty-minute set at a citywide "jam at the beach" night. Where could you go to get your toes out into the community? We tell our kids' church, "Christianity that stays in these four walls isn't real Christianity at all." Think of the ministry opportunities all around you, perhaps just a phone call away: school assemblies, nursing homes, veterans' meetings, mall holiday shows, and so on. If you and your team work on your gifts, what doors may God open to let you minister for Him? That's exciting!

As you start to put together your childrens' ministries service teams, and plan your service lineups and outreach ministries, make sure you always work for quality by preparing well. Here are a few strategies for upping your level of excellence when using illustrative methods:

(1). Plan to put a lot of time and effort into your services. Please understand this word of advice and caution: nothing of great value comes without hard work. One person reading out of a book really is easier. It's little to no prep or set up. But the results will reflect that effort. You truly get what you put into it. To really create a kids' church service that incorporates teams and illustrative methods will cost you time, effort, set-up, and preplanning.

(2). Meet with your team often. Rehearse. Set high expectations. I advise meeting every week with whoever is helping you with the service. Ask big. I have my rehearsals on Saturday afternoons from three to five o'clock. We start every rehearsal with prayer and discuss which creative elements we will be working with next. Then we work hard on our puppet songs, or dance numbers, kids worship, or dramas. On Sunday morning hits we are ready to rock. And the expectations are high. They know they have to be there early before service to pray and warm up. I expect good attitudes, full attention, and great interaction with our target audience: the kids. It is up to you as the leader to set the tone of quality and excellence in everything your teams do. Another of my rules is, "If you don't rehearse, you don't go on." This is followed by, "If you're not ready with that element (song, illustration etc), we are waiting until next week so we can practice it more." Set the bar high, use each other's creative gifts, and constantly strive to do better. Don't limit God. You will be shocked by what He will do when you have the courage to step out and try.

(3) Collaborate and work as a team. You are aiming to take your team from being handed a script to one, making the video clip, and finding the right song. See the difference? I always reserve final say, but I love the free flow of ideas. Many of the best ideas over the past ten years have come from our youth, not me. You are much more effective planning as a team.

(4) Keep the focus on ministry, not performing. This can be an opportunity to teach our young leaders how to serve. This is where they learn to use their God-given gifts for Jesus, not selfishly. Egos get dropped to one side as they learn to work together as a team and love the kids. Right now their world, their culture is shouting at them, "It's all about you and what you want." You are teaching them, "It's not about you; it's about Jesus, and what He wants." Each week when our teams rehearse I tell them the same thing: "This is not about us, or making us a star. It is about Jesus; He's the star. This service is our gift to Him. And we don't give God our trash. Let's work hard to connect His kids to Him this week. Let's give our best and make something to make Him proud! If they leave saying only 'they were awesome,' we failed. If they leave saying 'Jesus is awesome' we won." These kids, teens, and adult leaders could quote that speech to you by now! It is not about perfection, or putting on a show, it's about getting across the message of Jesus Christ in the most effective way possible.

Now that you're convinced of the benefits to incorporating illustrative methods into your children's ministry, let's look at the more popular ones that children's leaders are using today.

1. Puppetry. About twelve years ago, I vividly remember sitting in an auditorium at a packed conference for children's pastors. The speaker

emphatically announced that "puppets are dead." His point was that puppetry is a thing of the past, and if you try to use puppets in ministry, you will only get laughed at. I remember shaking my head thinking, "This just doesn't sound right to me." Fast forward several years. By now you have probably noticed that a "puppet guy" won America's Got Talent, Sesame Street is still a top rated show, and *The Muppet Movie* was the number 1 film in America several weeks running. It made a ridiculous amount of money, and at the writing of this book, the sequel is about to come out. I think it is safe to say that the speaker at that conference spoke too soon. Having said this, I do want to give you a few tips if you try puppetry in your ministry.

A. Aim high. Please do not fall into the trap of saying, "It's just for the kids, and they'll never notice anyway, so let's just throw whatever up there." Wrong times ten. Children do notice a lack of quality, and it makes them feel less valued. This is going to mean rehearsing with your team before attempting a puppet song or character routine. That love of quality leads us to:

B. Get some training. There are some good books out there on puppetry and workshops at certain kids' ministry conferences. You and your team can learn the do's and don'ts of puppetry and get new ideas of things to try.

C. Start small. Your first week is probably not the time to debut a black light rollerblading puppet "rap off." (I did that once. It was awesome. And a bit scary).What about having a puppet help with your rules, memory verse, or fast worship songs? (Note: Because a puppet will take everyone's full attention in any room, do not use a puppet during slower worship songs, the message, or prayer times. Focus should not be on a puppet during those times!) A recurring puppet character gets instant attention and excitement from your group. This will also greatly increase their retention of what you are saying. I've used an elephant puppet who can't remember anything, an air-headed owl, and a mouse who sings opera. After seeing you using a puppet, more kids will want to join your puppet team rehearsals! That first time using a puppetin your service may be scary, but it's worth it! Remember, it's not about perfection. It's about doing our best for Him!

A note on ventriloquism, which I personally love for several reasons. I have the benefits of a puppet: full attention, better retention, without the equipment needs, like stage, curtains, and so on. This has been so handy on mission trips, in schools, and last-minute ministry opportunities. I just grab a puppet and go! I have several Bible stories memorized to fit with several themes. The main drawback of ventriloquism is how long it takes to learn. It has less to do with "throwing your voice" and more to do with creating a believable character with a believable voice. Character development and acting are even more important than lip control. If you notice, all the greatest ventriloquists from years ago had terrible lip control, but no one cared. They created characters that people still love to this day. After a second or two, no one is watching your lips. They are lost for a moment in the story and forget that this is a puppet. So work on your character and voice first. Then work on lip control, especially on the problem letters and letter sounds: *b, f, m, p, v,* and *w.* It helped me to record myself and watch it over and over. TIP: The best place I have found to purchase puppets at a great place is eBay! Surprise!

2. Black light. This involves using black lights and florescent paint, florescent puppets etc. to make parts of your service "glow." For example, you can use black lights to make a puppet song "glow" or even light up a fast worship song using singers in bright T-shirts. It's fun and it can be an affordable way to get your point across with a punch. Black lights can be purchased at Walmart for very little money. Set them up on music stands or chairs. Be careful with the cords; you'll need to tape them down to avoid tripping. Then pull out a black light puppet and prepare to make a memory these kids will talk about all week. I highly advise that your team rehearse and sharpen their basic

skills first, but after you feel more confident with puppetry, dance, and drama, try them black light. If someone in your group has an artistic gift, have them draw or paint on a poster board in florescent colors, and then light it up! Black light dance teams and black light puppet teams always draw a lot of visitors. One fast worship song we did included black light bubbles and light diffusing fog. (You can get these at www.froggies.com.) On one occasion I used a black light cross in a darkened room to illustrate that we are the light of the world, and we have to let our lights shine. Some of these kids recall that message ten years later (which makes me feel old). Kids are more visual now than ever before. For very little money, you can make your point in a way they will never forget.

3. Storytelling. Jesus is the master storyteller. Look at the parables and His sermon illustrations. Jesus knows the power of great storytelling. In fact, Scripture tells us, "Without a parable He did not speak to the people." If I asked you to tell me what you learned on your first day of second grade, or when you learned your first math problem, you may have trouble telling me that memory with a lot of clarity. But if I asked you to tell me a story you first heard in childhood, I bet you could think of one! Everyone has heard a story. Everyone has their personal history

and story to tell. Christians have the most important story to tell—the most important story anyone has ever told or heard, anywhere anytime.

A story touches the deepest part of us in ways a lecture never could. Around the world in every culture in every language throughout history, people have loved telling stories to entertain, teach, and preserve their history. Need to really get your point across? Tell a story!

If you are not sure how to start storytelling to your group of kids, don't tell them just any story. Tell them your story. Of course, use discretion and don't bring up things they are not old enough or mature enough to hear. But telling *your* story is of the utmost importance. In fact, Scripture makes it mandatory for us to tell the next generation what the Lord has done for us. In Deuteronomy 6, in some of the first instructions God gave His people, He emphatically charges the entire congregation with telling their children—the next generation—all the amazing things they saw God do for them. Unfortunately, these commands were not obeyed. We know this because Judges 21:25 says, "and then a new generation arose who did not know all of the works of the Lord, and so they abandoned the Lord—everyone did what was right in their own eyes. And the Lord rejected them." Our nation is full of people who have abandoned the Lord. Could it be that they grew up never knowing the works of the Lord? Could it be that so many of us are still in violation of God's command to "tell the next generation the amazing works of the Lord?"

Have you ever noticed, that in Matthew 11, when John the Baptist sent his disciples to Jesus to ask "are you the Son of God or do we look for another?" Jesus doesn't respond with a lecture, or twenty organized reasons why He is the Son of God. What He says is remarkable, "Go tell John, what you see and what you hear. Tell Him the blind see and the lame walk and the dead are raised. And happy is he who is not ashamed of Me."

Don't just argue, tell the story of what you have seen God do. Has God done great and amazing things, answered prayers for you, for your church? Well, of course. But here's the bigger question. Do the children of your church and community know what God has done? Don't assume they do. Tell the stories and tell them well. Tell them often. Not sure how to do storytelling well, or just want to improve your skills and impact? A lot of colleges and universities have storytelling classes you can take for credit or for audit. Practice is the best way to improve!

Storytelling is a vital part of other illustrative methods, such as costume characters, puppet skits, drama skits, and ventriloquism.

4. Costume characters. This is as simple as having someone dress up as a character (Bible character, full body puppet, silly creature) and having them interact with your audience. Some great starter ideas would be: (A) Have two silly costume characters greet the kids as they enter the area (we use two florescent monkey costumes). (B) Have a crazy funny puppet or costume character help teach the memory verse, (they will remember it far better that way!), take the offering, or help with fast worship songs. (C) Instead of just telling the Bible story, have costume characters come in and act it out. Or have a costume character tell it first person. One time, when talking about the life of Isaiah for our kids, we had a man in his 70s come in dressed as Isaiah and tell "his" vision of the greatness of God. It was powerful. (D) Get a box of smaller costumes ready and let some of the kids come up and act out the story. This is hands-down the best way to get them to remember that story forever (remember kinesthetic learning = 80 percent retention). A few words of caution: (A) Make sure to always clarify which stories are true. When acting out or telling a Bible story, testimony, or missionary story I always say, "and guys, this is a true story, it actually happened." Kids are exposed to lots of fiction from fairy tales, movies, and books. They need to know that, even though you may be using fun, creative methods, the stories you are telling actually happened. (B) Don't use costume characters during slower

worship songs, message, or altar times. Costume characters command a lot of attention by nature, and you need the focus on the most important thing, the reason you are all there—meeting with God. (C). Smaller children can be afraid of costume characters, especially ones with bright, dark, or garish makeup on their faces. Train your team not to "force" a child to come over to them. Try to find costumes that are as friendly and cuddly as possible. Early on in my ministry, I did an Easter drama for the main service with angels and demons. As soon as the angels in bright white makeup entered from stage left, three of the preschoolers in the front row began screaming and sobbing hysterically. I remember thinking, "And we haven't even brought out the demons yet." Needless to say it really put a damper on the morning. (D). You need to protect your characters. Children think of live characters as living cartoons or big stuffed animals and therefore incapable of feeling pain. Children's leaders complain that their costume characters get punched, kicked, squeezed, and stepped on. This may sound silly, but after the second time a greeter monkey got socked in the gut, I recruited a "bodyguard" to watch over my characters, especially if they are out greeting. They have bodyguards with the characters at Disney and Nickelodeon events for the same reason.

5. Games. Kinesthetic learning (hands on) is best, so how can you get your kids up and moving without wasting a moment of the precious time you minister to them? Earlier we talked about not using any time in your service on anything not related to your topic. I highly suggest looking at your topic for a certain week and coming up with a game (sometimes one is provided with the curriculum) that reinforces your theme. I once attended an inner city church that did a great job at this. Their theme was "Fishers of Men; sharing your faith." So the game used a fishing pole over a curtain to "catch" fish using their verse of the day. All of the kids were talking about it as they left that day! I also suggest putting your game near the beginning of your service, to burn off their energy, or at the very end, in case it goes long. If the service goes short for any reason, I do not want worship, message, or prayer getting cut. To me, anything else— games, crafts, snacks—is expendable. Worship, message, and prayer are not negotiable. A word of caution: try to put yourself in the parents' shoes and imagine what they are seeing as they drop their children off and pick them up. At my last pastorate, I went to drop my kids off on my first Sunday. In the kids' area I saw chaos—screaming, yelling, pushing, crying—and then a sound speaker was knocked over. What I saw at pickup was even worse. Needless to say, that was the first issue I had to tackle. Try to avoid wild games when parents are dropping off and picking up. Keep

in mind that kids get hurt, but we need to do everything we can to limit injuries while they are in our care. I banned indoor "slam ball" in one small room and instituted other games instead. I personally have fun action worship songs going fifteen minutes prior to the service, so when kids enter, their parents see their kids jump right into an exciting worship service. I put the game, if I have one that week, right after fast worship or during the verse (see my sample lineup at the end of this chapter). Before using a game, ask yourself these questions: (1) Does it fit with and reinforce our theme this week? (2) Will we have time for it without cutting the essentials? (3) Is it wise and safe with this group of kids? (4) If a parent walked in during the game what would he or she think? Check online, especially Pinterest, for game ideas for your group!

6. Crafts. This is a weak area for me. I have never been good at crafts, and I don't particularly enjoy anything "craftsy." However, that kinesthetic learning is important and a lot of kids learn best through doing with their hands. My own daughter adores crafts. Her favorite Sunday services are the ones when she makes a "take home." Everything we talked about for the game section applies here too: (1) Is it relevant to our topic? (2) Do we have time? (3) Is it wise for this group of kids? (4) Will parents approve? Since this area is not my forte,

I find people who are gifted in this area to come in from time to time and do a special take home. One thing I really like about crafts is that the child has an actual physical reminder of what you said to look at throughout the week. Besides those included with your curriculum, you can find crafts and take home ideas at Pinterest, Oriental Trading, Dollar General, and Hobby Lobby etc.

7. Live action drama. There is a huge difference between reading a story out of your curriculum book and having it acted out live. Remember how live always trumps? If you get a chance to take a video or story and act it out live, go for it. Just remember to have your team rehearse. Many colleges have drama courses for credit or audit, and training can take your team to a whole new level. Keep dramas short, ten minutes maximum, and make sure they support your theme. I usually put funny dramas near the beginning and serious dramas right before altar call. I always watch it before it is performed, and if it isn't ready, we give it another week of rehearsals. Remember to make your motions BIG and use large props if you can. Instead of conversational chatting, aim to be like a living cartoon. Have your actors project, aiming to be heard all the way to the back of the room (you cannot always count on mics, if you have them). I highly advise taking your team to watch another team that is further along than yours, at a camp

or a conference, to get ideas. Having your team enter a fine-arts competition also raises your incentive and level of excellence. If done well, drama is one of the most powerful and effective tools in your ministry arsenal for Sunday mornings and outreaches.

8. Dance. I realize that some denominations and churches have reservations—even controversy—about dance, especially when used in ministry. I've heard a lot of objections from "dance promotes sexual activity" to "we are being like the world" to "this will tempt pedophiles to stalk children." While I understand the culture these objections are coming from, the reality is that almost all of these kids dance. Even elementary schoolers go to dances now. Their TV shows all include big dance numbers (think *High School Musical* and every show on Disney XD). Certain cultures thrive on dance as a part of their culture and their everyday story. While in Africa, I noticed that every get together with the kids included dance. It is as natural to them as breathing. Now, anyone who knows me knows that I can't dance. No seriously. Just ask my staff. Or anyone who has observed me. This traditional pastor's daughter couldn't dance to save her life. I even do my Zumba at home. All alone. In the dark. With the shades drawn. But when I realized the power of dance as a medium to reach kids, I found young people in our church who could teach dance to our kids. When our kids' dance team

opens the service with a bang, everyone is stoked, on their feet jumping, ready to do church. We set the tone with excitement, excellence, and expectation. I get the most requests from camps, malls, and other churches for our dance team to come in. Want a great place to start? Have a few dedicated kids rehearse the motions to your fast worship songs with style. This will take your worship services to a whole new level (just watch the Hillsong Kids live). You may need to find a talented person to work with your group on choreographing songs. YouTube, camps, and fine arts festivals are great places to get ideas. Make sure that any dance numbers support the overall theme, and that the dance moves are not anywhere near suggestive. I always watch every element before it goes on in front of children. If kids in your group are dancing inappropriately, don't overreact. They are imitating what they are seeing everyday on TV, the Internet, and at school. This is a great opportunity to talk about the difference Jesus makes in every area of our lives. Get your kids up and moving; it will increase retention and excitement, elevate your level of excellence, and decrease distracted fidgeting and wiggles.

9. Snacks. You may have already guessed that this is not one of my favorite service elements. Snacks pose major problems, including: (A) They can waste a great deal of precious time. (B) They can lead to

fighting among kids over who got what. (C) Snacks are a budget item that you may not want to spend. Could those funds better serve you in another area? (New worship CDs, for example.) (D) If that weren't enough to consider, parents are more and more unhappy and vocal about certain snacks. Parents have met with me to get me to sign a statement that their child will never have snacks with sugar, preservatives, red dye, caffeine, and so on. It has gotten difficult for teachers to figure out who can have which snacks when. Most importantly, there are food allergies and medical food alerts to consider (see chapter 8). This is not something we can overlook anymore. If you choose to do snacks, here are basic questions to ask: (1) Does this snack directly benefit our class? Toddlers get cranky from hunger at a certain point, and a snack is a great benefit to the whole class. I have a pre-K teacher who is a genius at making snacks directly support the whole lesson. When she taught on Daniel in the Lion's Den, each child made a Rice Krispies lion's head with edible decorations. It was a combination craft, snack, and take home. On top of this, she made sure it was gluten free, peanut free, dye free, and preservative free. The kids and parents loved it. (2) Will you still have time for worship, message, and prayer? Exactly how much time are we spending each week preparing, serving, eating, and cleaning up after snacks? (3) Is it safe? (4) Do we have budget for it? Always keep in mind that you and your team are there each week to touch lives for Jesus, and you only have one hour. Make it count!

10. Media. We are light years away from popping in a video, "entertaining" kids, or babysitting. Media pieces when used correctly are a phenomenal tool to communicate God's truth to our kids. Media clips should be short. I use one to two media pieces at five minutes apiece maximum. The goal is to not let media dominate or be a crutch. Kids already spend too much time on computers! Don't lean on or rely on media to be your service. Most media pieces are generic, impersonal, and some of your kids will tune out during them. Some great rules for using media in kids' ministry are: (A). No more than five minutes at a time. (B) Make sure the video clip goes with your theme for that day. (C) Always watch the video clip before you show it. Make sure the content is appropriate for the age group. No crudeness, no heavy slang, no references to subject matter that is too mature for children. Always keep in mind that parents have very different ideas of what is appropriate for their kids. And of course, you need to partner with parents, not flippantly upset them. One children's pastor I know ended up having a meeting with parents and the board because he said "darn" up front. I've also heard big blowups from using the words *stupid*, *dumb*, and *gun*, (thought they were promoting violence to

children) a SpongeBob reference, a Disney reference (parent that believes Disney is evil) and many more. Pick your battles, and don't do things just for shock value. Carefully pick illustrative methods that will uplift your service. You cannot eliminate conflict in kids' ministry. But you can cut down on it. My top places to get video clips are GodTube, YouTube, Sermon Spice, and ones I make myself. What things do I use media for the most? (1) Sermon countdowns. We bought professional sermon countdowns, and I love them. They get the kids excited for the service. (2) Baptism tutorials. (3) Offering challenges. (4) Announcements. (5) Verses. I do a segment called "Ask Ashton" where Ashton, a third grader, helps teach the memory verse. (6) Altar video. Sometimes I use a more poignant video to lead into altar time.

11. Worship team. Get some of your more enthusiastic kids up front helping lead the worship! Have them really rehearse those movements and songs. The big thing here is heart, smiles, and enthusiasm. I would rather have three kids so in love with Jesus and who love to worship with joy than two hundred amazing singers who just want to be stars. I have several kids on our worship team who cannot sing, but who dance, do motions, play a drum, or do a costume character to the music. Do not let just anyone jump on stage. Don't allow chaos, pushing, yelling, or fighting for mics. Have anyone interested apply (Sample application

at the back of this book). I find a place for everyone who wants to serve. They must first come to rehearsals, and get on the schedule. The children who are scheduled that day wear their ministry T-shirt so I know who should be on the stage. Keep working hard on this one, because a team of kids up front who are passionate about Jesus and worship will change the entire culture of your kids' church.

12. Guest interview. Invite a guest to your kids' church and interview them talk-show style in front of the kids. (A video of the interview, though not having quite the same impact, will also work.) Who should you seek out to interview? Who would the kids enjoy and benefit from hearing? Remember, you have not, because you ask not. So, don't be afraid to ask big. Since you cannot prescreen a live interview, try to make sure you know this person and that the content will not be over their heads. Here are a few ideas. (A.) Take some time to thoughtfully and prayerfully write out four to five questions ahead of time and send them on to the person you are interviewing so he or she has time to think about answers. Here are some questions I have used through the years: How did you know God was calling you into ministry? Tell us what God is doing in your ministry/life right now. How can we, a kids' church, get involved right now in ministry? Tell us about the best and worst parts of what you do for God. (B.) Keep your live interview to

only 20 minutes at the most and five to seven minutes for videos. (C.) Try to blend your interview with your theme for that day. For example, when we were studying missions last year, I brought in a vibrant young missionary skilled in kids' missions who had exciting stories of how God was using the money the kids were giving each week to change lives in South Africa. It was powerful. Remember: This is a chance for the kids to hear from another voice besides yours, confirming things you have already been teaching them. So who are the ideal people to interview? I highly suggest you use this opportunity to play team. Make sure you ask to interview your lead pastor and his or her spouse. Our lead pastor, an intelligent, highly intellectual speaker, surprised us all with his ability to connect and impact the kids. This was a great opportunity for the kids to realize they are part of the church now, not just in the future. Our church's senior leader got to see firsthand what God was doing in the kids' ministry at our church. Other potential interviewees: your youth pastor, worship pastor or leader, missionaries, your district or conference children's ministries leaders, a kids' evangelist, someone in your church that is from another country, someone just back from a missions trip, a leader at a local homeless shelter, or a children's hospital chaplain. These special interviews are times our kids have never forgotten and still talk about.

13. Mini field trip. What if instead of just talking about something, you took them there to see it? Kinesthetic learning, remember? There are some legalities involved in a field trip. You need liability forms signed by parents to take kids offsite (see chapter 8). I  suggest that for starters you try a trip close to home. With permission, on a weekend when your theme is giving or helping others, take the kids to see your church's food pantry or clothing giveaway areas. Being there makes it much more real. Does your church have a giveaway or donations box in the foyer? Show it to the kids and ask them how they can participate. One clever children's pastor, on a weekend about serving with humility, gathered all the fourth and fifth graders and had them wash all the windows in the church's cafe area. The kids had a blast, and everyone was talking about it. It caused such a buzz that the church launched a successful serving team that continues thriving to this day. I highly suggest taking your five year olds on a field trip the two Sundays before they graduate up so they can gradually acclimate to their new class. Same goes for your students moving into middle school. You may have already heard that there is a huge drop in numbers as children move from elementary into youth group. The

number of kids leaving church in that pivotal year of their lives is troubling; let's do whatever we can to do that hand off well. I have also taken the kids on "in-house" field trips for occasions such as observing water baptisms, communion, or a day of serving as door greeters. I have even seen children's pastors do scavenger hunts throughout the building and the lawn. Just make sure you think it through: Is it on topic? Is it safe? Is it worth the risk? In the end, nothing gets your point across better than taking them there.

14. Object lessons and illusions. In the same way that Jesus is a master storyteller, He is also fantastic at object lessons. Notice how in the gospels Jesus always used things, people, and situations that His listeners understood. Examples include: "If your son should ask you for a piece of bread would you give him a serpent?" "And He set a small child in front of them and said, "Whoever comes to Me must come as a little child or not at all." "Not finding fruit on the fig tree He cursed it and said 'may fruit never grow on you again.'" He uses common items: sheep, seed, bread, wineskins, and so on. Object lessons can be a powerful, memorable, and tangible way to get your point across. When picking an object lesson for your message, start with these questions:

- What would be memorable and interesting for the kids?

- What would be familiar and everyday for them?

- What would fit with our theme this week?

Rehearse your object lesson, even in front of a mirror to see how it looks. Not sure where to find ideas for object lessons? Your curriculum should have some ideas. If you go on social media with your theme, other kids' leaders may have posted cutting-edge ideas. Check Pinterest. It also has object lesson ideas. Object lessons should be visually powerful and help to teach your overall theme. You may even unintentionally challenge some of your leaders and the parents listening as well, because a well-done object lesson speaks powerfully across the generations.

I do also do illusions, lots of them. Several of them involve fire. Some churches feel that if you use the word *illusion*, you are promoting magic and witchcraft. I always explain to our audiences that both the power of God and the power of evil are real. And I talk to them about avoiding anything that smacks of spells, witches, talking to the dead, and so on. I also tell them that all TV magicians and illusionists are good actors, and that there is a trick to what they are doing. I tell them that when I do an illusion to make a point, there is always a trick to it—a trick that I am not going to tell them. And likewise, God will do amazing supernatural things around the altar that are not a trick and that are all about His power. I always look for opportunities to talk to kids about real versus fake. Fairy tales=fake. Bible and other history stories = completely real. Kids are forming and solidifying the major beliefs that will become the basis for the rest of their lives. It is so important to help them learn the distinction between real and fake. But I have not had any issues with children knowing that my illusions are tricks. It definitely gets their attention, and they do not forget my point—ever. Once I was talking about the obstacles in the way between us and a deeper relationship with God. I set out all kinds of obstacles—police tape, road cones, fencing, and "flash paper flame poles" (kiddos, don't try this at home. I made them myself). As I gave my message, I painstakingly crawled, squeezed and kicked my way through the obstacles to the huge cross I had set up on the other end. My point was: Stop making excuses and go after God. "Draw near to God, and He will draw near to you" (James 4:8).

Below is a sample lineup from that service. We currently use ProPresenter and Planning Center now for all service lineups, and I love it. But before that, we wrote everything in outline form. Here is that weekend's service, with creative element flow, in outline form.

Theme: GO AFTER GOD. Don't let anything stand in your way.

Preservice: 5 costume characters greeting, countdown on the screen. Lights, foggers, screens, stage and chairs in a cool new design

1. Saddle Up Your Horses Dance Number (Fine Arts Team)

2. Live Worship Fast Songs

        A.

        B.

        C.

3. Ask Ashton Media clip (we made in house): two verses "See Me and you will find Me, if you seek Me with all your heart." and "Ask and it will be given to you, Seek and you will find, knock and the door will be opened to you." Matt 7:7

4. Announcements and offering Pastor Laura

5. Media clip from Matt 7:7 (from YouTube)

6. Trish and Patti (ventriloquism) ASK, SEEK, KNOCK

7. Object Lesson- (when P. Trisha speaks) tons and tons of obstacles on the stage that she will climb over, under, through- flash fire

8. Message (P. Trish and P. Laura will take turns with this- P. Laura may go whatever direction the Lord gives her to go!! :)) P. Trisha- Go

after God. Don't let any obstacle keep you from Him. Not bitterness, or fear, or guilt.....Go after God no matter WHO doesn't like it!

9. Altar Worship-

    A.

    B.

10. Split to small groups, curriculum lesson #11 pp113-131

11. Ending game

12. Proceed to checkout- hand out take home "magnifying glass" to remind them to keep seeking after God

This is the basic outline we do every week, no matter which curriculum we are using.

(children in Africa raising their hands to accept Christ in our outreach)

We may change the format a lot, use different elements, and vary the schedule. But we always aim to do a "church service" based on having an encounter with God. We want these kids talking about Him all week. And creative elements help us do that. This didn't happen overnight. It has taken years of hard work, training, and most of all prayer. Many times, when we didn't know how to best present a certain topic, we prayed and asked the God of all creativity to make us creative, and He has helped us. Don't be intimidated or limited by the creative elements listed here. These are just some of the tools that children's leaders are using to engage kids in their services. So what will happen when you take that curriculum, pray over it, rehearse with your team, and instead of plopping out cold SpaghettiOs, you cook up a masterpiece of God's grace for your group of kids that they can't wait to jump in and experience? I urge you to take a chance and find out. Sometimes the hardest part, is just taking that first step. I believe in you.

"Every children's leader should have a 'story in their pocket,' at all times. Meaning, a well-rehearsed story, ready to go. You never know when you are going to need it."

—Rev. Daniel E. Rector, Chair of Children's Pastoral Ministry, North Central University (ret.)

Wait—what about Kerri?

Hey, hey, so glad you were able to come talk to me today. Here have a seat right here. I know you are really strapped for time today after church. It was a very busy morning over our whole church today, including the kids' ministry. Okay, I can see right now you are pretty nervous. Listen, really, you didn't do anything wrong. Relax and just breathe, okay? I didn't call you in here to chew you out. Quite the opposite actually. I needed to say something important.

Kerri, I wanted to thank you, personally, straight from this pastor's heart for all you are doing. I wanted you to know that I see your amazing heart for these kids. When you first sat in that chair across from me in this office and we talked about the kids' ministry, I only asked you to "fill in the gap" for three months. And obviously, that hasn't happened. Seven months have gone by now, and you have graciously and faithfully kept working hard for our kids.

I wanted to you know that I see how much our church, including the kids' ministry, is growing. Those seven children who were water baptized this morning had such amazing testimonies! Parents and volunteers are loving the new curriculum, and as pastor, I am so excited and relieved to finally be receiving positive feedback about our kids' programs. By the way, at our board meeting last

Tuesday, we were able to accept about 85 percent of your proposed budget, and we'll definitely be talking about that. But we were so very impressed by the quality and the thought you put into it. I am also so happy to see so many new leaders and new families getting plugged in and receiving the training they need before and during ministry to our kids. Well done, Kerri. One of best things I am hearing from parents and volunteers is that you are a great communicator. They always know what is going on and feel like they finally have input in the future of this ministry. And you definitely have brought some quality leaders on board! I personally feel, as our church board does, that you have made such great strides to make our kids safe. These were improvements we had never thought of. I admire your tenacity on behalf of our children. And our kids' church services, of course, are at a whole new level. I just love seeing kids serving in ministry and counting this as their church, and better yet, families serving together. I loved getting to see all of this firsthand last Wednesday night for your volunteer event. Thank you for inviting me. By the way, I appreciated your willingness to do that Easter thing for us on such short notice without complaining. Sorry about that but you and your team really impressed us by how you came through in a pinch. And I know it was difficult dealing with that whole Fletcher family fiasco with such grace. That was a rough one, but you handled it well. And we won't even bring up young Baxter's little stunt at the parade. I think we all learned a few lessons there.

Yes, I did get your email about needing to have another recruitment push in the next three months. Didn't we just do one of those? Really? We still need more people? Huh, I guess this is going to be an ongoing thing as we keep growing. I wanted to ask you about launching a special needs ministry for our kids. Can you do some research on that? We have no idea where to start, but it is something it looks like we need to get going on. How can we address the needs of families with special needs kids? We have two new families now coming with kids with autism. How do we minister well to them and to other kids that God may send our way? I'll admit I don't have all those answers. Let's start looking into that.

It is also becoming apparent that we need to do some problem solving on our current space problem on Wednesday nights. What was that? Oh yes, I agree, it is a very good problem to have. How can we better use our space now, while planning for future growth?

Now don't cry! I didn't want to overwhelm you or make you feel bad. One day, one Sunday at a time, Kerri. I just wanted to plan ahead, that's all. Oh, good. Happy tears. That's good. Kerri, I don't know that all kids' leaders get to hear the things they need to hear from their senior leader. And I'm sure I've been guilty about that too. You and your team need to hear, "Thank you, for serving our kids. Thank you, for loving our kids. I see all the hard work you are putting in and I appreciate it. All those sleepless night were worth it. What you are doing is so important. You are doing an amazing job. What can we the church do to better support you, our leaders, our families and our kids?

And just know that if I do forget to say it, or don't say it enough (and I cannot ever express these things to you enough) that Jesus sees and He is so proud of the legacy you are leaving. Please don't give up on Him, don't give up on our church, don't give on these kids, and don't you ever give up on yourself. Thank you for all you do.

Kerri, the second thing I called you in here to talk to you about it this: The congregation and I no longer want to "go find someone else" to run our kids' programs. We believe you are the person God has given us to do it. Not a perfect person, but the perfect person for us. Perhaps you were called here for such a time as this. You have improved so much, learned so much, come so far over these past seven months.

Kerri, will you consider staying on in ministry to our kids?
Will you, Kerri? Kerri?
Will you?

"Dear children's leader, thank YOU for taking this journey together with me. I hope you are encouraged today in all you do. Thank you for all YOU do for Jesus and His kids."

"All my thanks, and my love to my family, friends, and mentors whose prayers and encouragement made this God-dream a reality. I am so grateful." Love Pastor Trisha

COMING SOON TO A BOOKSTORE NEAR YOU:

"Your Children's Ministry from Scratch: The Enormous Sequel" featuring:

A. Special Needs Kids' Ministry in Your Church

B. Launching that first big outreach step by step (VBS, musical, etc.)

C. Surviving conflict in ministry and living to tell about it

D. Creating a dynamic kids' worship space